BUSINESS, GOVERNMENT & SOCIETY:

MANAGING CORPORATE PUBLIC AFFAIRS

GEOFF ALLEN

First published in 2025 by Real Publishing
www.realpublishing.com.au
Text © Geoff Allen
Images © Centre for Corporate Public Affairs
Graph, p.127 © Charles Fombrun

Business, Government & Society: Managing Corporate Public Affairs
ISBN: 978-0-6456811-9-2

A catalogue record for this
book is available from the
National Library of Australia

NATIONAL
LIBRARY
OF AUSTRALIA

REAL
PUBLISHING

BUSINESS, GOVERNMENT & SOCIETY:

MANAGING CORPORATE PUBLIC AFFAIRS

GEOFF ALLEN

Geoff Allen, one of Australia's foremost experts in the field, has written an authoritative and informative text on this important business function, rich with examples and case studies and full of valuable insights both for corporate public affairs practitioners and for business managers.

The Hon Paul Fletcher MP, former Federal Minister and
former Director, Corporate and Regulatory Affairs, Optus Ltd

Geoff Allen – true pioneer of corporate public affairs – has written this insightful, accessible book to show us how integrating management of these issues blows up dreaded silos and adds significant value for companies.

Professor Jennifer J Griffin, Quinlan School of Business,
Loyola University Chicago

At a time of rising challenges to the corporate sector, this timely and important new book skilfully covers all the key areas of corporate public affairs, from government relations to issues management to stakeholder engagement. It is written by one of the most experienced thinkers and practitioners in the field in Australia. It is highly recommended for corporate practitioners, government policy makers, business association leaders, interest groups, academics, and students.

Professor Stephen Bell, University of Queensland

Companies need a holistic approach to their critical non-market stakeholders. This book, authored by a practitioner who has done it all, fills an important gap in material for specialist executives, general business managers and management educators.

The Hon Warwick Smith AO, company director and former
Federal Minister

I am convinced that the management of social and political issues must be part of the normal corporate decision making process and the future of the corporation. We can do our sums, excel in production and marketing, fine-tune our cash flows, and manage people effectively – but we still fail badly if we do not properly address social and political issues.

Sir Arvi Parbo AC, former Chairman BHP Ltd, WMC Ltd, Alcoa Australia

GEOFF ALLEN, AM

Geoff Allen has spent five decades at the intersection of business and government in Australia. As a Commonwealth public servant, he became senior advisor to the minister for labour, federal treasurer and leader of the opposition in the 1970s.

He was then appointed senior research fellow at the Melbourne Business School (MBS) where he pioneered the teaching and research in business-government relations in Australia in the 1970s. He became deputy chairman of MBS for ten years and for twenty years continued to teach in MBA and executive programs.

Allen was co-founder of the Business Council of Australia (BCA) and designed its structure and modus operandi. He was foundation CEO during Australia's Hawke-Keating era of major economic reform. During his time at BCA, Allen played a key role in creating business unity on vital national issues.

He subsequently formed the Allen Consulting Group which led a new wave of outsourced public policy research, advising senior government and business clients. He served as chairman on several Commonwealth and state government advisory councils, including the Trade Policy Advisory Council and the Australian Statistics Advisory Council. He was a member of the government's Foreign Affairs Council and Prime Minister's Community Business Partnership, national chair of the Committee for Economic Development of Australia (CEDA), and director of several public companies in the mining and tertiary sectors.

In 1990, Allen founded the Australian Centre for Corporate Public Affairs which has been the catalyst for thought leadership and professional development for corporate public affairs management in Australia for more than thirty years. He was also Asia-Pacific regional editor of the *Journal of Public Affairs*.

He received a Centenary Medal for services to international trade and was appointed a Member of the Order of Australia in 2009 in recognition of his contribution to business-government relations and public affairs.

A Note on Nomenclature

While the term 'public affairs' has been common, a survey of major companies by the Centre for Corporate Public Affairs found that a majority now refer to the function as 'corporate affairs'. The terms are interchangeable but, in general, corporate affairs will be used in this book to refer to the function and its practitioners.

CONTENTS

INTRODUCTION

The social and political environment is crucial to the nature and performance of business. It is shaped by a complex array of institutions, interests and ideologies involving governments, activists and citizens in general, and in turn is influenced by the activities of business itself.

Governments are deemed responsible, to the extent of their capabilities, for establishing the regulatory framework and economic conditions in which businesses operate. However, the general public also influences companies significantly, whether through local community actions, activist movements, or the political process.

Accordingly, businesses, particularly large companies and those in industries most exposed to social and political challenges, need to be attuned to the expectations of governments, as well as the evolving values and demands of the community. Understanding and adapting to these non-market forces is important in developing business strategy and effective day-to-day business management.

Corporate public affairs has been defined in a variety of ways, each with a subtle difference of emphasis. As this writer has defined it:

> *Public affairs is the professional practice within organisations concerned with the analysis and management of social and political issues affecting the organisation. It encompasses public policy, government relations, stakeholder and issues management, and strategic communications including media, employee communications and corporate reputation*[1]

A leader in the profession, Wayne Burns, notes its higher purpose:

> *Public affairs at the highest level is a leadership function that manages risk and creates opportunities, shaping an organisation's*

---

strategy and influencing the social and political environment to deliver beneficial outcomes.[2]

While there have been longstanding academic traditions in management functions like finance, accounting, marketing and regulatory economics, the recognition of corporate public affairs as a professional function within academia has been slow. Academics have struggled to develop theoretical frameworks that add up to 'disciplines' such as those in other more established management fields. This has hindered the placing of corporate public affairs management beside other management disciplines in our universities.

A partial reason for its slow recognition as a management function in academia could be explained by Rice University's Duane Windsor:

Public affairs remains in search of identity, conceptualisation, theory, effective organisation, best practice, and social legitimacy... There is no 'grand theory' of public affairs – no integrative or overarching framework.[3]

Windsor suggests that corporate public affairs is not a uniform discipline but lies at the interface of multiple disciplines that are linked to different elements of the corporate public affairs task and contribute to its intellectual roots. Longstanding teaching and research in many of these separate disciplines includes:

- Business in societies and business ethics (including corporate citizenship and social responsibility, corporate social performance, theory and stakeholder management),

- Communications and public relations,

- Ecological systems (including appreciation of corporate and stakeholder impacts on natural ecological systems and the issues generated by them),

2   Burns W (2008) *Corporate Public Affairs – Asia Edition*, Vol 2, No 2

3   Windsor D 'Theories and Theoretical Roots of Public Affairs', in Harris P & Fleisher C (Eds.) (2005) *The Handbook of Public Affairs*, Sage Publications, London

- Economics (including collective action, public choice theory, transaction cost theory and game theory),
- Organisational sociology,
- Political science, and
- Strategic management (including agency theory, behavioural theory of the firm and integrated strategic management theory).

Academic attention to corporate public affairs management as a discipline was significantly enhanced by the launch of the *Journal of Public Affairs* and 'handbooks'[4] of corporate public affairs published in 2005 and 2017. These were followed by the *Palgrave Encyclopedia of Interest Groups, Lobbying and Public Affairs*.[5] Journals such as *Business & Society* and academic books covered relevant topics. Academic authors, however, reflect a huge diversity in the conceptualising of the function across the globe and, when considered as a whole, leave the impression that there are wide gaps between academic theory and corporate practice. One exception is the development of programs like 'managing in the non-market environment' or the equivalent in some of America's top business schools.

To understand the practice of corporate public affairs management in major companies, Professor Jenn Griffin, then at George Washington University, noted three waves of empirical research leading to a more practical understanding of the corporate public affairs management task.[6]

The first, 'foundation building', was early work on business government relationships involving several surveys that explored the role of corporate public affairs in firms in North America.

---

4   Harris P & Fleisher C (Eds.) (2005) *The Handbook of Public Affairs*, Sage Publications, London and Harris P & Fleisher C (Eds.) (2017) *The Sage Handbook of International Public Affairs*, Sage Publications, London

5   Harris P, Bitoni A, Fleischer C & Binderkrantz AS (Eds.) (2022) *The Palgrave Encyclopedia of Interest Groups, Lobbying and Public Affairs*, Switzerland

6   Griffin JJ (2017) 'Empirical Study of Public Affairs: A Review and Synthesis' in Harris P & Fleischer C (Eds.) *The Handbook of Public Affairs*, Sage Publications, London

The second wave explored, often through case studies, how firms organised and deployed their resources in the political arena through political involvement, building upon managerial capabilities and issues management. Further work on political management tactics was complemented by studies into the political environment of business with an emphasis on regulated industries, and on the global regulatory environment and international institutions.

The third research wave she identified, 'blurring the boundaries', is a recognition of the increasingly broad and integrative concept of 'corporate public affairs'. This approach, which has become the dominant model in Australia, is now being more widely adopted in the US and elsewhere. This is a blurring of boundaries between corporate public affairs, political strategy, public relations, sustainability, communications and reputation management in business, government and society relationships.

While there are differences between companies because of scale, organisational philosophy or industry, there is a common view among Australian practitioners about the role of the corporate public affairs practitioner. They see the function as developing (in conjunction with top management), holding and communicating the company's core narrative and related themes to all internal and external stakeholders; responding to business needs with activities determined by business plans and well-articulated issues priorities; facilitating cohesion and consistency in external relations policies, reputation and behaviours; maintaining cohesive and seamless relations with non-market stakeholders; facilitating deep understanding in companies of the risks and opportunities arising from the social and political environment of the company; and working closely to educate and assist line management in the pursuit of these objectives.

Business, Government & Society: Managing Corporate Public Affairs

This book was prepared with the encouragement of The Australian Centre for Corporate Public Affairs, the professional body for corporate public affairs departments in Australia and its region. It draws on the author's experience as a political advisor, business school academic, business association CEO and management consultant. Many examples of issues and practice cited here have emerged from his consulting experience. The book also draws on information and advice from practitioners who undertake leadership of the function in major companies.

It is intended as a basic primer or foundation text for new entrants to the field, use in undergraduate and professional development programs, and as an introduction to the function for general managers and other corporate specialists whose understanding and cooperation is essential to managing in the social and political environment.

CHAPTER ONE: THE DEVELOPMENT OF CORPORATE PUBLIC AFFAIRS

Corporate public affairs has evolved from disparate activities to what is often an integrated business function, interpreting the social and political environment to guide company actions, creating opportunities, protecting interests and influencing stakeholders.

Jason Laird, Executive General Manager, Corporate Affairs, National Australia Bank Ltd.

In the middle of the twentieth century, businesses were valued in the western world as employers, creators of wealth, and nation builders. Governments looked to business leaders as essential to post-WW2 reconstruction, and aggressively sought foreign business investment. Bank managers were considered benign and avuncular pillars of society. Miners were celebrated for creating new wealth, and pharmaceutical and chemical companies were feted for their contributions to health and living standards.

From the 1960s and early 1970s, there was a burst of change in social and political attitudes and the consequent reputation of big business, much of it influenced by developments in the USA.

A better educated and more affluent middle class became increasingly critical of business and its profit motive. Books that challenged corporate reputation during this time populated bookshelves in the English-speaking world.

Vance Packard's book, an assault on advertising[7], was widely read and discussed. Other popular books included John Kenneth Galbraith's attack on consumerism[8], and the military-industrial complex[9]; US activist Ralph Nader's expose of consumer issues in the automotive industry[10]; Rachel Carson's dramatic book on the environmental impacts of pesticides[11]; and Anthony Sampson's tome on the oligopoly and political power of oil companies in 1975.[12]

Protest techniques, honed in Australia as well as the USA in response to the Vietnam War, energised activists whose agendas

7   Vance P (1957) *The Hidden Persuaders*, Penguin

8   Galbraith, JK (1958) *The Affluent Society*, Houghton Miffen Harcourt, Boston

9   Galbraith, JK (1967) *The New Industrial State*, Houghton Miffen Harcourt, Boston

10   Nader, R (1965) *Unsafe at Any Speed*, Grossman Publishers

11   Carson, R (1962) *Silent Spring*, Houghton Miffen Harcourt, Boston

12   Sampson, A (1975) *The Seven Sisters: The Great Oil Companies and the World They Shaped*, Viking

challenged business. New radical groups formed to confront environmental issues. One example is Friends of the Earth (FOE), an Australian group of young activists formed in 1975 initially to combat uranium mining. Movement Against Uranium Mining (MAUM) was a middle-class breakaway group with a similar agenda.

Companies were confronted directly by demonstrations, media campaigns and the use of activist shareholder resolutions at annual general meetings, a tactic pioneered by US activist Ralph Nader. In 1975, to enable standing as shareholders, 250 activists each held one Western Mining Corporation share and three cent dividend cheques were proudly displayed on the walls of the FOE office.

The election of the union-affiliated Australian Labor Party (ALP) in 1972 saw a shift in focus from class and the socialisation of industry to an aggressive 'quality of life' agenda conducive to the new activist demands made of business. The media, with its self-appointed role of ombudsman and guardian of the public interest, caught the mood and imposed more critical scrutiny of business behaviour.

Responsive politicians deepened their capitalist view of business as an instrument of public policy, leading to an avalanche of regulations affecting nearly every aspect of business activity. Governments increasingly focused on environmental and consumer issues, as well as the rights of small investors, which further intensified regulatory intervention.

Surveys showed that trust and respect for big business fell dramatically through this time, reinforcing these pressures.

Many in business felt aggrieved and misunderstood. Business leaders defended themselves against attacks on their industries by citing statistics on employment, exports, tax contributions, and corporate philanthropy, as well as scientific arguments to assuage fears about public health and the environment. These efforts proved futile as much of society had lost trust in business and many individuals felt their wellbeing was threatened by corporate activity.

Rather than confronting the causes of criticism, business initially misinterpreted these challenges, seeing them as left-wing assaults on the capitalist system. It sought to defend capitalism through the formation of groups such as the Institute of Public Affairs (IPA)[13], the short-lived Free Enterprise Association[14] and similar organisations.

Industry associations, including chambers of commerce, attempted to win young minds through 'economic education'. Schools were inundated with literature lauding free enterprise; business assisted teachers in curriculum development; and resource materials were co-produced by business and educators.[15]

Mainstream business associations, led by traditional old-boy networks, kept their focus almost exclusively on industrial and trade matters and were slow to address this changing socio-political environment.

New thinking about how managers should respond to these challenges had been developing in academic circles in the United States, and was introduced into research and teaching in major US business schools in the 1970s. The influential Stanford Graduate School of Business professor, David Baron, saw the need for management to adapt to the new environment[16] and introduced a compulsory MBA course on managing in the non-market environment. Other academics, like David Vogel at Berkeley and James Post at Boston University, brought these issues into teaching in their management programs. The Melbourne Business School taught Australian MBA students innovative courses on business-government relations and the social and political environment of business in the mid-1970s.

A catalyst for the development of a professional corporate response to these developments in Australian companies was the bringing together of communications and government relations executives in major companies into a new organisation, the Centre for Corporate Public Affairs in 1990. Executives in communications and government affairs across industry and geographic divides came together in a

---

13 The IPA was formed by business leaders during the Second World War to defend society from socialism in post-war reconstruction. It continues to be the most prominent right-wing think tank in Australia.

14 The Free Enterprise Association, also established by the captains of industry, commenced with a flourish but lasted only several years.

15 Allen G (31 March 1976) 'The Capitalist Counter-Offensive', The Age

16 Baron D (1993) Business and its Environment, Prentice Hall, New Jersey

series of retreats to discuss public policy in the late 1980s under the auspices of the Allen Consulting Group. It became a quasi-professional association with a focus on best practice and professional development. Its membership consists of the public affairs or corporate affairs departments of most of Australia's large public companies and some government enterprises.

By the early 1990s, forward-thinking business leaders had come to appreciate the need for new management approaches to their social and political pressures. Launching the Centre for Corporate Public Affairs, Australia's most prominent business leader at the time, Sir Arvi Parbo, said: "Management from the grassroots to the boardroom should be thinking about these (social and political) issues intrinsically when business plans are being made as well as in the everyday processes of managing."

As community attitudes and heightened community expectations were rising, companies were not well resourced or structured to respond.

Prior to the 1980s government matters in companies had been largely led by technocrats recruited from the middle levels of the public service. Their role was centred largely on damage control, defending company interests from regulatory developments with low-level interventions. Former journalists employed in communications and public relations roles were preoccupied with solving media problems and promoting sales and the company image.

Through the 1980s, demands from a more sophisticated and economically literate audience saw a shift in public policy advocacy. Cosy networks of business and government insiders gave way to the demands for publicly argued, evidence-based policy. This led to a more open, sophisticated and research-oriented approach to government relations in companies, and different leadership competencies for business associations.

The political science concept of legitimacy was applied to thinking about business and the so-called 'legitimacy gap' arrived early in the language of corporate affairs. It was a precursor to the current idea of 'social licence to operate'.

These changes gave rise to a more structured approach to social and political issues, to understand their causes, and respond appropriately. Tools and techniques were developed to assist in managing these issues from early identification through to their resolution.

The increasing challenges of external non-market forces led to a greater appreciation of non-business stakeholders, those people or groups who had an impact on, and were impacted by, the activities of a company or industry. Stakeholder engagement for both defensive and constructive purposes became a fundamental management function.

In tandem with these developments, corporate thinking about charitable activities became more strategic. The concept of corporate philanthropy, which involved making disinterested contributions to worthy causes, evolved into a more deliberate approach known as corporate community investment. This approach seeks mutual benefits through partnerships with strategically selected community organisations.

This shift was closely linked to the corporate response to increasing demands for greater accountability regarding social and environmental impacts. These demands took centre stage in the late 1980s when environmental sustainability became a central issue, and they morphed into more general demands for social as well as environmental responsibility. More recently, attention to corporate governance was added to this list of concerns and the more common summary nomenclature changed from corporate social responsibility (CSR) to environment, social and governance (ESG) and to corporate 'purpose' which embodies goals beyond markets and money.

The 1990s saw a burst of attention to the issue of corporate reputation in all its economic, social and market dimensions. Reputation came to be understood as an important non-tangible asset and a competitive issue. Companies were faced with a new preoccupation with reputation rankings. Understanding, influencing and responding to a company's reputation became an important focus for corporate executives.

The increasingly challenging external environment for companies has led to greater sophistication in media management and corporate communication tools. Rapid changes in media technologies led to adjustments in strategies and vehicles for communications. In recent decades this has been complicated by the 24-hour media cycle, hollowing out of traditional media and the emergence of social media and resultant democratisation of information. The ongoing developments in artificial intelligence are presenting new challenges.

At the same time, a shift has occurred in internal communications from a focus on corporate cohesion and morale – as well, of course, the dissemination of important operational information – to a more strategic activity. A focus on staff engagement and two-way communication deepened as companies came to further appreciate the value of staff input to management and alignment with corporate strategic objectives.

Many external issues have political and government dimensions as the community in general and activists in particular seek regulatory intervention to influence or control business activity. At best practice, the government relations specialists in companies became less defensive and more creative in influencing public policy and, where appropriate, sought opportunities to creatively align corporate objectives and the requirements of governments.

Recognising the need to manage external non-market issues holistically, companies have integrated their external relations and internal communications functions under a single professional corporate affairs team or a company-wide community of practice. It is well understood that most non-market issues encompass overlapping media, reputation, community, staff, regulatory and political dimensions, all of which feed into each other and require holistic strategic responses.

Some companies manage regulatory affairs outside the corporate affairs portfolio, which may be appropriate where they are deeply technical and require specialisation beyond mainstream government relations professionals.

When contemporary corporate affairs was emerging, investor relations was an integral part of the portfolio, largely because of the centrality of the media to that task. As markets and shareholder relations became more complex, however, a new specialist investor relations function arose within corporate finance departments.

Where it is not organisationally integrated with investor relations and regulatory affairs, investor relations issues are managed in close cooperation with corporate affairs which provides communications support.

As socio-political issues have become increasingly important to the success of companies, the corporate affairs function is playing a more strategic role in corporate planning and decision-making. The most senior corporate affairs executives now commonly sit at the second or third level in corporate hierarchies and close working relationships with CEOs are the norm.

During the first decade of the 21st century, the integrated corporate affairs function had attained a professional identity. It became accepted that its frameworks and tools were necessary to enable the environment and issues to be managed in a systematic manner. Most of its current concepts and management tools had also been established, although developments in, and management responses to, social media and artificial intelligence are still rapidly evolving.

CHAPTER TWO: GOVERNMENT RELATIONS

In many sectors, the most successful companies regard management responses to the political environment as core business rather than a peripheral or low-level support activity. Politics and government can no longer be a spectator sport for major companies.

Matthew Percival, former Group Executive Public Affairs and Chief of Staff, AMP Ltd

Studies of major companies have found that government and regulatory stakeholders are more likely to impact the value of a business than other stakeholders such as employees and investors. This varies, of course, between industries, with some more subject to regulation and vulnerable to government decisions than others.

Prior to the 1970s, relations between business and government were conducted largely in what might be called an 'insider game', where deals were made between 'old-boy' networks with business leaders (and sometimes with unions) without much external scrutiny or publicly argued justification.

Several key factors have contributed to policy making becoming more sophisticated and open to debate.

While governments had been active in areas of economic activity, such as trade, taxation and industrial relations, their attention from the 1970s turned to a range of social and other issues such as the environment, consumer and investor protection, monopolies and oligopolies, gender equity and occupational health and safety.

By the early 1980s, a new breed of young, bright and economically trained public servants assumed leadership of economic departments. They worked towards a free market and evidence-based economic order and away from deal making with closeted industries. The development of economic modelling, both inside and outside of government, on the impact of policies had a major effect on advocacy and policy making.

While mateship between individuals and political incentives for politicians will always drive some subterranean deal making, these changes drove the shift towards contestable advice and an 'outsider game' of external advocacy and scrutiny. Businesses were now obliged to make a rational case in the public interest for their policy proposals and argue them openly with evidence. Governments, under greater

How to Make Canberra Listen

In July 1982, *Business Review Weekly* journalist Robert Gottliebsen told the story succinctly, under the heading 'How to Make Canberra Listen'.

> *When Malcolm Fraser suddenly announced the depreciation concessions last week, he ushered in a new era in the Canberra lobbying industry. The three-year campaign to change Australia's attitude to depreciation had not been fought on the traditional old-boy basis, but with an expensive and detailed research program. The opponents of the depreciation concessions in Canberra, led by Treasury, were confronted with masses of statistical evidence, which caused them to lose the initiative. Over the years the Canberra bureaucratic machine has become skilled at dealing with the old-boy network and putting down proposals as 'industry garbage'. Cases argued to politicians over scotch at the club had normally lacked detailed back up.*

Gottliebsen was referring to a campaign by the predecessor of the Business Council of Australia (BCA), the Australian Industries Development Association (AIDA). It involved a major survey of business tax and subsidies in fifteen countries. The data was analysed by the AIDA Research Centre on a methodology it had borrowed from an OECD economist.

However, establishing a rationale for good policy is not always enough. Governments need motivation to act and supporting business objectives can sometimes be politically inconvenient. Effective advocacy therefore requires selling the policy rationale for decisions on the one hand, while creating the political incentive (or reducing the disincentive) for them to pursue it on the other.

scrutiny, were under a heavier obligation to justify their decisions publicly, based on objective criteria.

To meet the need for publicly contestable policy argument, industry associations became more sophisticated, and a new breed of economic and policy consultancies sprang up to undertake research and prepare submissions on behalf of companies and their industry representatives. This was illustrated by the appointment of more academically trained association professionals in the late 1970s.

This approach was summed up by the declaration of the CEO of one association that it is "working towards fully matching in quality and sophistication the advice the government gets from its public service".[17]

The notion of 'political capital' plays an important part in government relations. The term refers to a store of credit that can be earned or spent, or goodwill that can be gained or lost. Politicians require political capital to maintain their standing and legitimacy with electors and other relevant parties. Accordingly, governments are reluctant to spend their political capital on behalf of unpopular business causes. One political leader, for example, told a company that had mismanaged its relationship in its community that he would not overrule community demands affecting the company even though he was sympathetic to its cause. His exact words were: "Don't expect me to waste my political capital on you when you have stuffed up." On the other hand, business can work to create conditions that make it easier for politicians to be supportive. As one prime minister said to a group of business leaders after being lobbied on a policy that would create political challenges, "OK you've convinced me of the policy; now go out and make me do it!"

As the march of regulatory intervention continues and government activity deepens its impact on business, the need for effective government relations has become more compelling. This is especially the case for the larger and more heavily regulated sectors, such as resources and infrastructure, with their long investment-to-payoff lead-times that depend on predictability and therefore a stable political and regulatory environment.

Government relations can be a competitive weapon for companies within sectors. Early warning of emerging government action can facilitate timely responses that enable strategic advantages over less prepared competitors, and winning policy arguments against a competitor can give competitive advantages. Consider the case in the automotive industry where a company with advanced technology for environmental control sought to win regulatory preference over its competitors by promoting the mandating of standards that better suited them. Good standing with government also helps competitive access to, for example, minerals or forestry resources when one company is seen as a developer of choice, while those with poor relations or reputations are left without.

Companies that are more advanced in their understanding of the significance of effective government relations invest more heavily in their capacity to deal creatively with governments. The attitudes of company leadership, especially the CEO, are critical to the ability of the company to reach its potential and to use government relations as a competitive tool. US practitioner and academic Robert Healy observed:

> *CEOs can be laggards who play catch up on external issues, reluctant participants, or political entrepreneurs with social and political advantage as a priority. These characteristics broadly reflect the stages in the evolution of public affairs to corporate leadership positions. Entrepreneurial first movers place a positive value on political participation...[they]...believe as an article of faith that governments, politics, media and social media are rationally exploitable ....[they]...have made investments in political resource capacity and have risk tolerance to exploit that capacity.*[18]

18   Healy R (2014) *Corporate Political Behaviour: Why Corporations Do What They Do in Politics*, Routledge, New York

Companies that opt for a low profile and choose not to invest in government relations proactively are less likely to attract political or activist attention, which may work in non-controversial industries. However, they can miss political and policy intelligence about emerging developments that could affect their plans and strategies, as well as opportunities that come from government policies and activities. In addition, they risk having to respond reactively, late in the life cycle of issues when they have little or no influence. They limit their ability to correct disinformation, frame their issues, build supportive coalitions, or deter government policy from creating unintended consequences. At their inception, several major infotech companies like Microsoft and Meta (formerly Facebook) that did not appreciate their political vulnerability suffered by not having an affirmative political culture and they were compelled to make significant late adjustments to their political preparedness.

Small and medium-sized companies are unlikely to employ specialist government relations executives. However, they may have politically active or well-connected leaders with access and influence. In general, most small and medium-sized companies can best be heard and informed in their collective strength through industry associations where they benefit from the scale of resources collectively deployed.

THE GOVERNMENT RELATIONS PROFESSIONAL

As noted, changes to business-government relations led to a rising professionalism in the business sector. This includes changes in the way companies approach the task of government relations. Before these changes, a small number of large and more protected companies employed government relations managers who operated at a relatively low transactional level, remote from strategy and core business activities. Where a dedicated government relations function existed in companies, it was invariably in the protected manufacturing industry or one of the few industries with a high degree of economic regulation. These jobs were typically staffed by former middle-level officials from government industry departments and their main tasks revolved around defending a tariff, pursuing a dumping action against importers, or ensuring the most favourable by-law application or sales tax exemption.

In the new environment, major companies began to employ specialist government relations executives with a higher level of experience in politics and public policy.

Understandably, larger companies and the more highly regulated industries such as resources, finance and utilities were the first to employ more inhouse resources to work on public policy and government relations. Former senior politicians and executives from the higher ranks of the bureaucracies joined companies to perform these roles.

As other chapters in this book illustrate, a broad range of social and political issues in the non-market environment, including public policy and regulation, are closely intermeshed. They can be influenced by many business' stakeholders – customers, employees, investors, the media, communities – which means regulatory and public policy issues need to be managed holistically. Accordingly, unlike in many countries such as the USA, government relations in Australia is normally an important sub-function of broader corporate affairs teams, and often the head of the corporate affairs function leads government relations.

Beyond sophistication in corporate affairs issues, it is very important that these government relations executives have a deep understanding of their business' other issues, its economics, its technologies and its marketplace. They should also be able to demonstrate to government actors they have internal legitimacy and authority. In many cases, however, it is appropriate for CEOs, business unit managers or technical specialists to front government interactions to support their government relations executives.

Another important role for a corporate affairs employee is to be advisor and coach to other executives, and to ensure the organisation overall is educated in politics and regulatory affairs. It is not uncommon for other managers to have unrealistic expectations of government and distorted views about government processes and protocols that can led to counterproductive outcomes.

Information is Currency

Assisting governments with useful information helps companies and associations become the 'go-to' source of information of value to government. Objective information about business operations, markets or technologies that assist policy makers to do their jobs is the currency of constructive relationships. Trusted relationships are helpful to understanding government motives, the issues that are important to them and matters that are currently under consideration.

BEST PRACTICE

It is important that companies have clear, proactive and achievable objectives for policy and regulatory outcomes rather than simply reacting to regulatory developments and the agendas of others. To be most effective requires a clear focus on what is most important to the company, including sleeper issues that might suddenly surface and work proactively to mitigate areas of vulnerability. This clear focus enables companies to remain ahead of the game, to be creative and, where possible, set agendas for policy and regulatory developments.

To maintain a constructive and proactive role in government affairs, appropriate relationships need to be established, where possible, with politicians, public servants, regulators and those who influence them. The most effective relationships require familiarity through personal contact. Trust should also be established and maintained through integrity, honesty and openness about the company's agenda.

Relationships are sustained by the perceived value of what the company can bring to government agents. Most policy makers and regulators are keen to learn what is happening in business and the marketplace and are happy to receive objective information relevant to their policy or regulatory task. Reporting on interviews with government relations practitioners, University of Queensland academic Professor Stephen Bell et al reported:

> *Most respondents thought that governments had become more interested in engagement with business, giving rise to the growth of 'pull factors' from government in the form of ongoing requests for information, advice, expertise, and participation in policy networks and advisory roles. This activity is referred to in the literature as 'access goods' whereby business provides needed goods to government in return for enhanced access to government, enhanced credibility, and perhaps increased influence.*[19]

Educating people in government, through trusted and helpful information about the marketplace and issues of their concern, also helps to inoculate them from perceptions of business that may be distorted by issues adversaries, political propagandists, their own ideological biases and the academic myopia that exists in some government agencies. A successful outcome is to become the 'go-to' source for useful information as government views and policies are being developed.

An obvious vehicle for building a mutually constructive relationship is to offer briefings on issues relevant to government agendas and to assist in providing information or market-based insights. This is effective if the information is seen to be disinterested and when it is not easily obtained elsewhere. Provision of internal company briefing documents, where they can be shared, are a costless example. Different styles and focus are appropriate for different levels in government, ranging, for example, from half-day seminars for middle-level public servants to snappy ten-minute discussions with documents to leave with ministers. Officials are also usually pleased to hear from international experts from multinational companies if their expertise or experience is relevant.

A corollary to this is the value of not approaching government with problems without some constructive and feasible suggestions to resolve them. Opening dialogue with some positive ideas demonstrates a wish to find a solution that can be accepted by both parties. To do so, it is necessary to understand what lies behind a government's approach to an issue.

Governments are rarely internally monolithic, and the motivations and circumstances of various government actors are not always transparent. They certainly cannot be reliably learned from what they say publicly. Governments can be divided by the direct interests of individuals and factions with complex incentives. The mandates of different departments often lead to competitive internal priorities. Regulators, bureaucrats, and ministerial advisors, as well as those outside on the edge of government who are influential, bring different mindsets to the resolution of issues.

A deep understanding of these motivations and pressures can facilitate alignment and positive-sum outcomes with key government actors. Optimising alignment may require acceptance by companies or industries of second-best solutions, or whatever is feasible given the imperatives of politics and public policy. Without this understanding, corporate leaders are prone to taking positions that are logical and compelling to themselves, but not to government actors or their constituents.

In one classic case, the advice of corporate affairs personnel that governments would have difficulty in approving coal seam gas developments, was dismissed by managers who thought it only logical that jobs and tax revenues would trump activist positions. Consider also the marketing manager who wanted to launch a fruity alcoholic mixer for the youth market when pressure was building against alcohol advertising, or the manager who wanted to close regional offices in the electorate of the fiercest parliamentary critic of the company as an election loomed.

Several government relations specialists have moved from company to company and across sectors. It is important, however, that in each company these specialists seek to embed best practice in process and culture so that effective government relations practice is sustained in those firms.

OTHER CONSIDERATIONS

Hospitality can be used effectively to make introductions and maintain connections. However, some in government are sensitive to potential criticism for accepting hospitality so certain guidelines should be taken into consideration. Companies frequently offer plant visits, which can be particularly useful for, and appreciated by, local members of parliament. Plant visits need to be interesting or have a particular relevance, and should provide an opportunity for building acquaintance, briefing or making a case to government. These visits also provide an opportunity for more relaxed discussion on issues and the establishment of trust away from the frenzy and short-attention spans that characterise the working places of ministers and backbench politicians.

Exchanges of personnel between companies and government can be effective in educating company executives about government and its processes, and to bring that knowledge back to the company. They can also assist governments to better understand business and the economic environment. An effective example was the secondment of a Treasury officer to the offshore marketing office of a major resource company, which gave the government important insights into the commodity markets on which future assessments of their revenues are based. These exchanges are difficult with politicians, but not impossible.

Governments are open to co-sponsoring projects with business, especially research projects in which there is a mutual interest. Some industry associations have sponsored research within government at arm's length where they believe the product of the research will be of benefit. Opportunities for co-sponsorship extend to exhibitions, conferences, communications and community projects. As well as their intrinsic value, all provide a useful means to build relationships and earn goodwill.

Regardless of its motivations, a government will have to justify decisions in terms of public interest, while some companies seek responses solely on the grounds of their own needs. Therefore, effective business advocacy should consider the public interest as the basis for its rationale.

While a rationally defensible case in the public interest is necessary, it is sometimes appropriate to pursue it in a low-key manner. However, positions will more commonly need to be argued publicly, with the media used to promote issues or build public legitimacy for company

Parliamentarians in Industry

Following a UK model, the Business Council of Australia, in cooperation with a supportive minister and shadow minister, arranged a program in which high-potential backbenchers from the major parties were paired with big companies. Mutual obligations included a specified number of days over a two-year period in which the politicians would sit with the company to observe their decision-making processes, technologies, financial arrangements, and interactions with customers and investors. Company executives were invited to observe at close quarters the activities of the politicians. More than a dozen politicians from both sides of the aisle – who all went on to assume ministerial roles – participated in the program while it lasted and reported finding the experience valuable.

positions. The publication of sponsored research, for example, can draw attention to the need for reform or to emerging challenges for an industry and its stakeholders.

There is a natural tendency to focus on political parties in power at the expense of other relevant actors. Even where there may be no immediate prospect of a change of government, it is important to develop and maintain relationships across the political spectrum, and to pursue an educating role with the opposition as well as with independent members of parliament. Opposition parties with limited resources take positions on issues and develop policy in anticipation of their turn in government, which provides an important opportunity for corporate affairs executives to influence future policy and reform. Also, independents and minority parties can of course wield significant bargaining power on legislation. Apart from the value of advice, this earns gratitude and goodwill, and facilitates access that might be critical at a future time. With considerably fewer resources, independents can also have a great appetite for ideas and information that companies can share.

At the same time, it is critical for companies and their representatives to resist becoming embroiled in the political agendas of political parties or factions. It is not uncommon for politicians to seek to use an unwary CEO to endorse their position on a controversial matter in a way that can have political consequences for the company.

Efforts to influence the political agenda can be undertaken with subtlety. For example, it is not uncommon for companies or industry associations to poll a politician's electorate on an issue they are pursuing if they think the results might have an influence.

Participation in government advisory bodies is a useful means to ensure business perspectives are on the table and provides an opportunity for business participants to better understand government thinking and priorities. Often, appointments to advisory bodies are nominated by industry associations, but they can also occur through other established networks and relationships built on trust.

Association engagement also provides an opportunity for contact with government and is an important vehicle for business managers to gain a better understanding of government. This is discussed further in Chapter 4.

LOBBYING

Much of the public perception of lobbying is determined by popular representations of the political processes in the US. There, professional lobbyists in specialist consultancies or law firms are active in representing company and industry interests directly in Washington and state capitals. This is different to models that exist elsewhere. More commonly, those referred to as lobbyists, or in Australia, 'political consultants', are facilitators of company advocacy rather than representatives undertaking advocacy on a company's behalf. They provide assistance through introductions, arranging appointments, monitoring activities, and providing political and public policy intelligence and strategic advice. This can be a useful adjunct to direct corporate activity, particularly for small and middle-sized companies with limited resources. However, where possible, governments strongly prefer direct interaction with company executives.

In Australia, public suspicion of the malevolent influence of lobbying, reinforced by some distasteful cases, has led to the establishment of some light regulation, including codes of conduct and the registration of lobbyists. This is mainly focused on transparency, requiring the registration of persons making representations on behalf of third parties, notification of client names, and notification of ownership of lobbying entities. These requirements do not include corporate government relations staff, or the staff of industry associations, charitable organisations or community interest groups who are all are exempt.

In addition, concern over the role of former politicians, political staff and senior officials with privileged information in the initial period after leaving government, has led to restrictions. For eighteen months, for example, federal ministers are not permitted to engage in lobbying on issues in which they had been engaged prior to their departure. Political staffers and Commonwealth officials are likewise restricted for twelve months.

Federal and state integrity commissions are particularly concerned with inappropriate influence on government. In cases where abuses have been found, this has led to censure and even custodial sentences.

PARTY FUNDING

Funding political parties in election campaigns is a controversial issue across the globe. Perceptions have been distorted by the significance of this issue in the political process in the USA. The rules on funding political parties vary from country to country. In Australia, significant public funding is made available to parties, and the level of funds raised from private sources is not a good predictor of political outcomes. The public rationale offered when companies donate has been to facilitate the democratic system, but no doubt they are also motivated to engender good will, and in cases where funding is not equally disbursed, to help the election of the party with policies favourable to their business.

Regulation of funding has been light and focused on transparency, although different jurisdictions are approaching reform. At both federal and state levels, anything above a relatively small amount of funding must be disclosed and the information is published. Trade unions, but not other partisan third parties are required to disclose.

Reportable donations by companies include the aggregation of modest funds paid to attend events, such as dinners with politicians and party conferences. A major trend in public companies, has been to make no contributions at all, except for participation in these activities.

The major parties at the national level recently introduced reforms that increased the level and timeliness of disclosure and established annual caps on what can be received by candidates and party administrative units, compensated by increased public funding. Independents and small parties opposed the changes they claimed would discriminate in favour of elected incumbents and the major parties.

Government Relations – Tales From the Field

These guys came into the minister's office and pulled out a slide show on the company's product range, market capitalisation, debt structure and so on. Didn't get to any issues we were interested in. After fifteen eye-glazing minutes, the minister excused himself for a division and made sure he didn't get back till they had gone. His first comment was, 'Whose arse should I kick for that?'

Ministerial private secretary

You wouldn't believe it but [the CEO] came into my office and ranted and threatened me politically if I didn't give him what he wanted. I was remarkably polite, but you can imagine how much help he got from me after that!

Cabinet minister

I gave them a heads-up about what was going on, how to present their case, the sort of things to say to the minister and what their chances were. They blabbed indiscreetly to the minister about what I had said, and I got a 'please explain' ... it was not very nice! You've got to know who you can trust.

Departmental assistant secretary

My boss was sucking up a bit when he told the minister that the opposition's policy would seriously hurt the industry. The minister quoted him directly to attack the Opposition during Question Time in parliament. He let himself be used. It was naive and I hope he learned from that.

Government relations practitioner

When I've got time, I am always happy to help people understand how things work, how to approach things, and what we need from them... and, if it is not too sensitive, what is going on. It saves us all time and it helps us do our job if they are informed and know their way around.

Public servant

I was really grateful to him for sending me his company's internal briefing on the oil market. I was just preparing a brief for the minister on petrol pricing. He occasionally sends me useful stuff, for example, on global markets or emerging technologies.

Public servant

A high-profile businessman accepted an invitation from the Opposition party to head up a government committee to advise on infrastructure policy if they were elected. Despite assurances, the party let this be known and the CEO and his company received less favourable treatment from the existing government.

CHAPTER THREE: INDUSTRY ASSOCIATIONS & COALITIONS

Associations are formed to combine resources and leverage. Companies join in pursuit of pre-competitive interests in areas including public policy and regulation, standard setting, enhancement and protection of reputation, promotion of products, and in some cases the provision of services. They provide a comparatively neutral political sphere for companies to pursue policy outcomes without attracting direct retribution from issues adversaries.

Gerard Brown, Group General Manager, ESG, Australia and New Zealand Banking Group Ltd

A significant percentage of corporate affairs activity for business in Australia is undertaken by industry associations. They perform a variety of functions, but the focus of this chapter will be the corporate affairs aspects of the association role. Corporate affairs practitioners are frequently recruited from companies to lead associations and many of their secretariates appoint corporate affairs specialists to research and pursue political and regulatory positions and to enhance the reputation of their industry or profession. The mindset and the skillset required of association executives parallel those of corporate affairs executives in major companies.

Associations are large in number and diverse in composition and activity. There are good reasons for companies and professional firms to come together. Most obvious is the strength that comes in numbers. The aggregation of resources and power of companies in associations enables research, debate and external communication that would not be feasible for individual firms.

Dialogue within associations facilitates industry cohesion on issues of importance and educates members about the social, political and, in some cases, the marketplace environment in which they operate. They provide a source of intelligence on regulatory and political developments that affect their members.

Associations also provide a means whereby best practice can be transferred between companies. Many provide statistics and a range of commercial and industrial services that assist particularly small and medium-sized members. The large membership in business and professional associations is a testament to their value.

Some industries have several sub-sector associations, for example those that operate in federal structures or those in an industry with distinct industry sub-sector policy committees. Any of these can exist separately in organisations at a regional, state and national level. They may or may not be affiliated into broader peak bodies within sectors or seek to represent business in general. National organisations such as commodity associations are often affiliated with international bodies representing their industry globally.

Several associations originated as employer organisations with a principal focus on industrial relations. While industrial relations remains a major issue for many, its relevant significance has lessened with the decline of centralised bargaining and industrial arbitration. Industrial relations issues re-emerge, however, when government pursues changes to the industrial relations system.

The building products, processed foods, chemical and plastics industries, as well as the metals sectors, for example, have a strong focus on developing and marketing their commodities in domestic and export markets. Some associations facilitate collaboration on technical matters, provide training and professional accreditation, set standards and industry self-regulation, and provide insurance and industrial advice. Some provide accreditation, professional development and other services.

Associations representing specific sectoral interests are in large part obliged to respond to all of the sector's significant issues. Others can be more selective and concentrate on a narrower group of priorities. With all this diversity it is not surprising that there is no 'one size fits all' approach to the leadership, structure and modus operandi of associations.

Governments value the opportunity to consult and advise associations and their members, and look to them for sector representation on advisory, and in some instances, regulatory bodies. It suits governments to have these vehicles. They lessen the cost of providing information to an industry and enable governments to more readily claim legitimacy in stakeholder consultation.

As small and medium-sized companies, and small groups or practices in the professions, are unlikely to have in-house corporate affairs practitioners they have a greater dependence on associations than larger companies, with their own well-resourced corporate affairs departments to monitor and advise on public policy and regulatory issues and to represent them to the public and policy makers.

One reason larger companies join associations is to influence the behaviour of others in their industry. Governments regulate industries rather than individual firms. Numerous examples show that reputations of industries as a whole can be impacted by the bad behaviour of only a few, and lead to regulatory intervention affecting all companies in an industry. To this end, most industry specific associations have adopted standards and codes of behaviour, with non-compliance often leading to censure, financial penalty or expulsion. Industry codes of conduct are dealt with more fully in Chapter 8.

ASSOCIATION MANAGEMENT

The management of industry associations has several challenges. Foremost amongst them is the need to stay effective while dealing with conflicting internal interests and policy preferences.

Within associations that include multiple sectors, for instance national peak bodies, considerable differences about policies or priorities arise. Examples might be tax policy, where retailers may have a different attitude to other sectors on the appropriate balance between levels of sales tax and direct company taxation. Differences can exist between hydrocarbon-producing sectors and those seeking preference for renewables or between protected domestic industries and importers.

Firms within sectors compete with each other and, as discussed elsewhere, reputation and government relations can be competitive weapons. For example, if one company in an automobile industry association is in a different cycle of product development from its peers and can get an edge in fuel efficiency, it is in that company's interest to promote a regulatory standard that disadvantages its competitors.

Even where there are no policy differences, there may be competition for association attention and resources. An oil and gas association, for example, might be divided by those prioritising the needs of offshore development and those wholly engaged in onshore fracking.

Scale can be a divisive factor. Within the retail industry considerable policy aspirations differ between small local retailers and national or international retail chains. Different interests on shopping hours is one example. And large banks might be satisfied with higher prudential requirements than smaller financial institutions that are less able to accommodate them.

Where there are policy differences, there is pressure to resort to 'lowest common denominator' decisions. Conflict is avoided by not taking positions on debates where even a small minority of members disagree, which can be a critical constraint on the impact of organisations. This results in a muted voice or absence in debate on issues. It also disempowers organisations and renders less useful the company resources that are spent on them.

Where conflicts cannot be resolved in voluntarist organisations, it is important not to stifle a broad consensus with a small group veto, but to allow a safety valve for different opinions. Accordingly, it should be deemed acceptable for a member in good standing to say without sanction, "On this matter we have a different position to our industry body."

Some associations have accommodated their differences by establishing internal sub-groups on specific issues. Sub-groups can fund their own research, and state their views where interests are narrow or positions are different. This can be an effective way of ensuring efficiency in the use of resources while still leveraging combined strength on the normally larger number of objectives held in common. Examples have been importers versus local manufacturers, geographic divisions, or particular product/commodity sub-groups within a larger industry organisation.

An important balance in associations is needed between the demands of members to focus on short-term and ad hoc issues while preserving a focus and applying resources to longer-term issues of greater importance. A common criticism of associations is that they are reactive and operate too late in the life cycle of issues. However, it is difficult for association executives under pressure to respond to a constant flow of issues affecting an industry at any one time as well as the demands of individual members. Ad hoc and immediate pressures make future agenda-setting a significant challenge for resource limited associations.

Policy structures need to ensure there is space for long-term analysis of the social, political and regulatory environment to identify issues early, set aspirational objectives and apply resources to advancing the interest of the industry.

When internal policy conflicts arise, experience has shown that reframing issues and extending resolution timeframes can facilitate a constructive path forward. While extended timeframes may seem suboptimal to those eager for quick results, they are generally less threatening to association members whose interests are impacted. This approach is usually preferable to facing resistance to change from these members.

Fee structures often cause disharmony amongst members. Fees are normally based on scale, for example the value or volume of production, or number of employees in a member company. The funding contribution of a few large companies will be much greater than that of a long tail of smaller ones. This gives rise to a common complaint from larger companies regarding 'free riders', the subsidising of smaller contributors, especially when they have different priorities. On the other hand, smaller members can resent the influence of larger companies who expect that their influence be commensurate with their contributions.

Apart from funding, large companies are normally heavily represented in association governance and, with their expert resources, can dominate committee and other policy work. In response to this, it is common to set minimum and maximum contributions and to ensure representation of smaller enterprises in policy forums.

Beyond policy priorities, the issue of scale is also exacerbated by different service needs. Larger organisations are more self-reliant in areas such as policy intelligence, training and industrial relations, while smaller companies look to their associations for these services. In some associations, the problem has been mitigated by the provision of fee-for-service activities in areas like enterprise industrial relations. This can help the free-loader problem while enabling the collective expertise and resources of the industry to be applied to the particular needs of smaller companies.

Policy conflicts and competition for resources have led members to exit associations and create smaller sub-sector organisational structures. The upside is clarity of focus; the downside is less external leverage, replicated overheads, and loss of critical mass for effective policy work and management. While continuing to feel the pressure to participate, the proliferation of associations and consequent demands for member time and fees has led to dissatisfaction, particularly by larger companies constantly reviewing their numerous memberships and urging rationalisation.

A criticism has been made over the years that some associations are too 'secretariate-driven'. This occurs when the professional staff has its own agenda that is unrepresentative of members' needs and positions. Secretariat capture – the secretariate running its own agenda – can be more apparent than real, and the perception of it may reflect the fact that individual company executives are happy to hide behind association officials to make their case, in order to avoid personal or corporate repercussions.

This alleged secretariat capture enables political leaders who seek to divide the industry to delegitimise inconvenient association positions. While pushing back against association advocacy, government leaders have also been known to lean on individual company CEOs to separate themselves from the positions of their associations. As one association leader observed:

> I've seen captains of industry kow-tow like limp fish to the treasurer. They go to water and back away from the industry's position. Politicians don't respect genuflection. And it certainly doesn't help the industry's case.

RELATIONS WITH CORPORATE AFFAIRS

As noted, a background or competency in corporate affairs is integral to the role played by the staff of association executives. However, tensions can arise between its practitioners and associations. This can occur, for example, when a senior executive of a member company is asked by an association to take a public position on behalf of the industry, which might have ramifications for the company's relationship with government, unions, interest groups or other stakeholders that the corporate affairs practitioner is trying to protect.

A sensitive dynamic also arises from the fact that association professionals are an alternative, and sometimes competitive, source of authority and advice to the company on politics and strategies for dealing with political or regulatory issues. To this end, some company practitioners have sought to undermine the standing of associations within their companies.

There are, however, many examples of very effective collaborations between company specialists and association executives, providing support for each other's activities. Where relationships are strong, corporate affairs executives can play a role in directly advising association staff and collaborating closely in the implementation of association agendas.

Some company executives in senior management teams seek to exclusively 'own' their involvement with associations when they represent their companies in association governance or policy committees. They can be reluctant, or just negligent, in canvassing issues and seeking support within the company before association meetings, for example. Some are also so close to their particular business unit or branch that they don't see the broader corporate position or stances taken in other parts of the company. There have been cases in which executives from the same company push conflicting positions to others in different associations or in different committees of the same association.

On the other hand, companies that use their corporate resources with planning and strategic intent can punch above their weight in association agenda setting and policy making. This occurs when their representatives participate in association committees and other meetings with a clear agenda, arguments and evidence, and have been well briefed on the politics and company aspirations. By winning influence within an association, companies can bias employment of association resources in their interests over competing priorities. Proactive companies get more value for their fees than those who are less active and strategic. An important task for the corporate affairs executive is to support their company representatives in these roles by working closely with them and providing a thorough briefing.

Advantages for management teams that become involved in associations include increased participation with peers from other companies on policy work; exposure to politicians, regulators and others; and better appreciation of the policy environment including challenges and opportunities that arise.

AD HOC COALITIONS

A less formal means of collaboration is an ad hoc coalition of companies or business leaders that pursues a specific goal or common interest. These have been formed when there are clear interests held in common, or when working through an association will blunt the effort or force policy compromise. They also enable companies to pursue particular interests with their own resources when an issue does not have sufficient priority for attention or resource allocation within an association.

These coalitions are often formed following discussions of issues amongst industry peers or on the initiative of an individual business leader. The advantages of informal coalitions include speed and flexibility in decision making, and the novelty of a fresh voice against the clutter of stale ongoing public debates. Strength is achieved by pooling resources for research, legal costs or to employ professional support. These coalitions can commission joint research, issue public statements, advocate through the media or collectively lobby decision makers.

They have even more impact when made up of disparate voices of leaders or organisations across sectors that would often be in opposition, such as with business and welfare groups, or farmers and environmentalists. Governments find it difficult to resist when traditionally opposing groups pursue a common policy. Historically, interventions by groups of four, five or even more respected voices have been influential in putting issues on the agenda.

Normally these coalitions coalesce around a specific issue and, whether it is for a one-off intervention or sustained program of scientific or policy research, there is an expectation that the group will disband once the specific mission is completed.

A Statement of Deep Concern

An example of a successful coalition was an intervention aimed at refocusing political attention onto economic policy. After a period of refreshing economic policy reform, business leaders sensed an atmosphere of government complacency was settling in. A group of twelve of Australia's most prominent CEOs proposed a ten-point reform plan to break a negative economic cycle and issued a proclamation titled 'A Statement of Deep Concern'. It stated:

> We are deeply concerned about the country's economic condition and the threat this poses to our community welfare... Political, business, union, community leaders and all Australians need to be committed to work together with a new sense of urgency to break the negative cycle.

Before the statement was released, planning discussions were held with progressive union leaders, who made constructive suggestions, and some reforming government ministers who agreed to champion the push in cabinet. One prominent union leader let his support be known in a major speech, in which he told ministers that progressive union leadership backed the statement. This support was facilitated behind the scenes by a public policy consultant directly employed by the group of CEOs. Press headlines, follow-up stories and strongly positive editorials led to sustained attention to the agenda. Other union leaders lent their qualified support in public forums.

Major business organisations were aware of and supported the initiative. They accepted that the approach made a refreshing change from their own regular voices and acknowledged that the direct intervention of business chiefs was key to achieving the desired impact.

CHAPTER FOUR: ISSUES MANAGEMENT

Issues management is the organised activity of identifying emerging trends, concerns or issues likely to affect an organisation to analyse their potential impacts and to develop creative, practical responses.

Professor John Mahon
Chair of International Business Policy & Strategy
University of Maine

Governments and public policy issues have always been important to the economic environment and regulation of business behaviour. However, new attention given to the impacts on a broad range of stakeholders in the 1960s and 1970s led to an increased focus in the community on business activity.

While significant corporate resources were allocated to technology, market research, and economic and financial forecasting, there was no sophisticated approach to understanding the associated pressures and trends or predicting their impacts on operations. Companies, however, became increasingly aware of their vulnerability to both social and political pressures.

A general interest in futures research emerged during the 1970s and 1980s as these changes began to take shape. Some in business adopted a technique called 'scenario planning' from military strategy to explore possible future situations and facilitate contingency responses. The articulation of a range of future scenarios was intended to provide a context for thinking clearly about the complex array of factors that may need to be considered in decision making.

Scenario planning included brainstorming trends, forces and events to establish 'possible', 'probable', 'best case' and 'worse case' situations. The risks and opportunities inherent in various scenarios and strategic responses were assessed to help managers develop flexible strategic plans that were adaptable to exogenous economic, political, social and environmental changes. Scenario planning continued to be used but did not take root widely as a mainstream business planning tool.

In the 1970s, a major strategic issues identification technique called 'socio-political vulnerability analysis and planning' was developed by General Electric in the USA.[20]

The first element was to create an inventory of social pressures on the corporation, as expressed by complaints made about corporate

SOCIO POLITICAL VULNERABILITY ANALYSIS

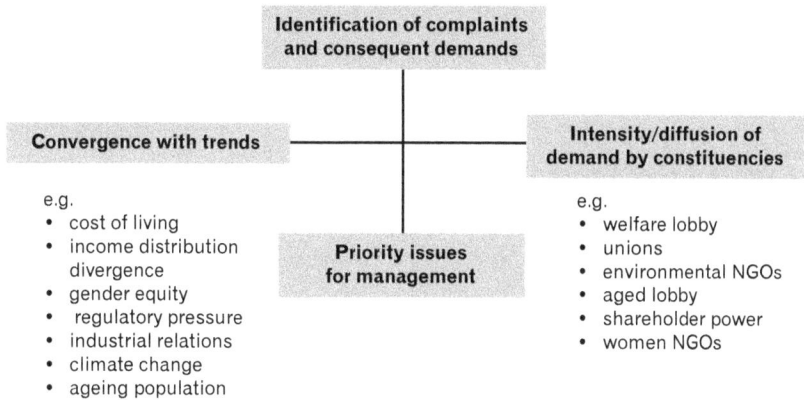

Identification of complaints and consequent demands

Convergence with trends

Intensity/diffusion of demand by constituencies

e.g.
- cost of living
- income distribution divergence
- gender equity
- regulatory pressure
- industrial relations
- climate change
- ageing population

Priority issues for management

e.g.
- welfare lobby
- unions
- environmental NGOs
- aged lobby
- shareholder power
- women NGOs

performance. The next stage was to identify the major demands being made in relation to those complaints (the range of solutions advocated) and to identify 'hazards' or adverse consequences for the company that might arise from an inadequate corporate response to those demands. The next stage was to assess the convergence of each demand with major social trends and the intensity of pressure behind the demand – the strength of feelings about the issue and power of groups pursuing them.

A numerical score is given to the convergence of pressures with social trends, and the intensity and power of the issues drivers, to determine a quantitative guide to the key issues the company should address. While the use of mathematical quantification seems unecessarily mechanistic, this combination of analysing trends alongside the potential influence of stakeholders and impacts on the business, foreshadowed current issues management practice.

In the mid-1970s, American consultant Howard Chase developed a standard framework to identify issues and corporate response.[21] By the mid-1980s, the issues management process he envisaged had become well established and was employed in many major companies.

An important concept in issues management is the 'legitimacy gap'.

20   Wilson IH (1974) 'Reforming the Strategic Planning Process: Integration of Social Responsibility and Business Needs', in Sethi SP (Ed.) *The Unstable Ground: Corporate Social Policy in a Dynamic Society*, Melville Publishing, Los Angeles

21   Chase H (1985) *Issues Management: Origins of the future*, Issues Action Publications, Washington

There is often a lack of full alignment between what an organisation does and what might be expected of it. The wider the gap between performance and expectations, the greater the loss of organisational reputation and legitimacy, which leads to increased demand for action to force changes in business behaviour (from community pressure or government regulation). For business, this externally mandated gap reduction means a loss of autonomy and the cost of meeting new demands and regulatory intervention

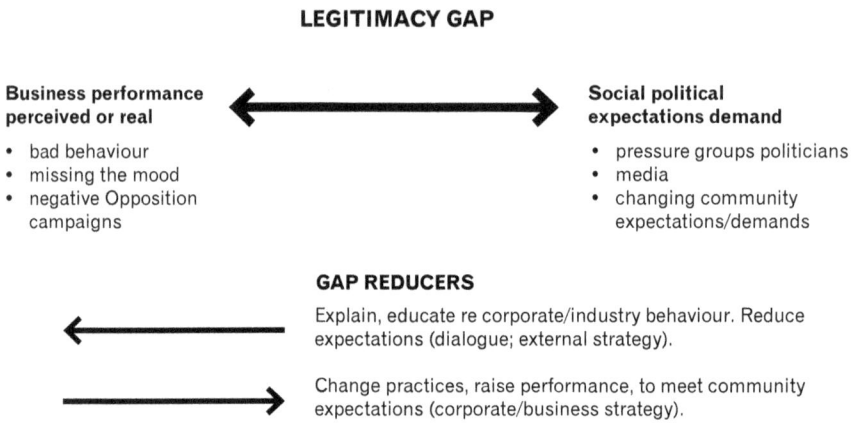

LEGITIMACY GAP

Business performance perceived or real

- bad behaviour
- missing the mood
- negative Opposition campaigns

Social political expectations demand

- pressure groups politicians
- media
- changing community expectations/demands

GAP REDUCERS

Explain, educate re corporate/industry behaviour. Reduce expectations (dialogue; external strategy).

Change practices, raise performance, to meet community expectations (corporate/business strategy).

The gap is pushed to the right on the diagram by the creation or expansion of expectations stakeholders have of a company or industry. These can reflect fundamental shifts in community thinking (for example on gender equity) or the demands of specific interest groups. These expectations can be exacerbated by politicians who sense votes on an issue pitching to electorates. Gap-wideners on the left of the diagram can be bad business behavior, either real or perceived.

In some cases, an appropriate corporate response will be a move towards meeting expectations, reducing the gap by accommodating change and adapting strategy and behaviour. Alternatively, it could be to engage in persuasive dialogue or advocacy to justify actions or reduce what are considered unreasonable or inappropriate expectations.

Another important concept underpinning issues management is the 'issues lifecycle'. This is a simple but useful adaptation of the product lifecycle to illustrate the process in which an issue emerges, is defined, matures, and is resolved over time.

Early identification of an emerging issue is crucial for developing an effective strategy to manage it. When, as is typical, management attention is paid to an issue late in its lifecycle, responses will necessarily be reactive and less effective than if they had been identified and addressed earlier. Issues that are not identified or are badly managed early in their lifecycle are more costly, or provide less useful solutions than if they were identified and understood at an early stage. They frequently escalate to demand more senior management time.

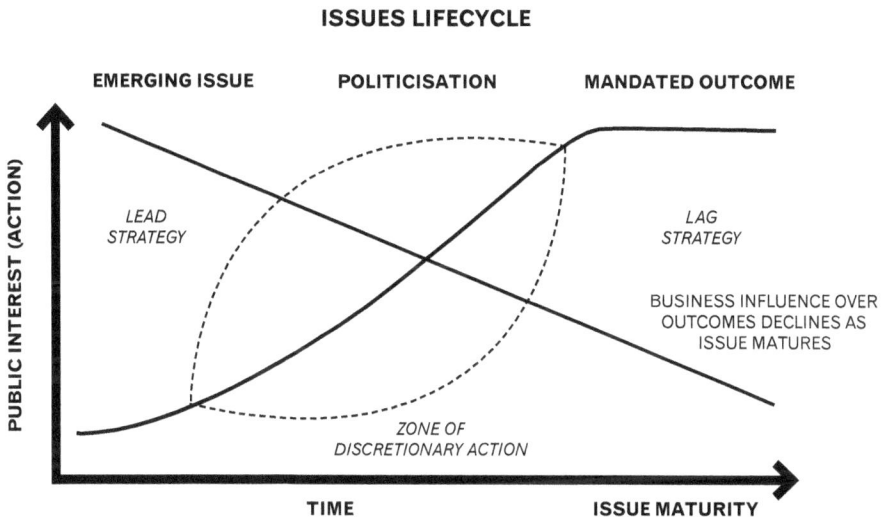

ISSUES LIFECYCLE

EMERGING ISSUE   POLITICISATION   MANDATED OUTCOME

PUBLIC INTEREST (ACTION)

LEAD STRATEGY

LAG STRATEGY

BUSINESS INFLUENCE OVER OUTCOMES DECLINES AS ISSUE MATURES

ZONE OF DISCRETIONARY ACTION

TIME   ISSUE MATURITY

It may be possible to contain an issue by adjusting corporate activities or actively engaging with stakeholders and government. However, as an issue gains more attention, a company's ability to influence outcomes declines. Demands become more clearly articulated by various stakeholders, options for resolution identified by others become entrenched. Consequently, management's ability to act diminishes, options for solutions narrow, and resolution becomes more challenging.

Having identified the emergence of an issue, companies can adopt either a lead or lag strategy. A lag strategy, just monitoring an issue without being proactive, will at times be appropriate. There may be no opportunities to influence outcomes; issues can abort or be deflected;

those driving the issue may be few or ineffective so that the issue subsides; circumstances driving issues might change; and outcomes may be so uncertain that the costs and risks required for proactive management outweigh the benefits. Nevertheless, these issues may warrant careful monitoring and their implications may need to be considered in strategic planning.

On the other hand, a lead strategy requires identifying desired outcomes and usually involves constructive stakeholder engagement or advocacy, which can help shape the resolution of an issue. A lead strategy could also include adjusting plans or operations, for example by discontinuing a product or business practice. A proactive or pre-emptive approach to issues management – getting ahead of the game – can have a critical impact on how an issue is framed, what stakeholders are involved and engaged, how the issue spills into other arenas, and other outcomes.

Framing an issue involves defining and shaping how it is understood, and winning the framing battle significantly increases the chances of prevailing on the issue itself. These framing contests are often central to public disputes, reflecting not only the competing ideologies of the parties involved but also their strategic communication tactics. Examples of framing include terms like 'murder of unborn children' versus 'women's rights' in the abortion debate, 'toxic waste dumps' versus 'prescribed waste facilities', or 'national sovereignty' versus 'local development' in foreign investment debates. Framing an issue is most effectively achieved early in the lifecycle. Reframing an issue as its lifecycle matures is difficult but possible, and may require a new approach, new arguments, and the engagement of a different group of stakeholders.

The choice of arena in which an issue plays out can also be crucial. Early analysis and a proactive approach can help a company rather than its adversaries select the venue to contest an issue. Companies can use the press, pursue legal strategies through the courts, solicit political or regulatory intervention, take the issue to opinion leaders or the local community, or place it in the hands of an industry association. It can be tactically advantageous to select multiple arenas to expose an issue position to a broader range of stakeholders, to heighten the sense of gravity and the importance of resolving an issue to advantage.

Early analysis of an emerging issue may also help a company influence the timing over how it is resolved, for instance by taking preemptive action to capture the initiative on framing and arena choice. This might be influenced by the electoral cycle or the readiness of issues' opponents to engage and compete. A lead and zinc smelter in a regional town heard that Greenpeace was planning to publish troubling data on lead pollution in the town's atmosphere. Before it could, the company effectively preempted the issue by publishing the data itself, together with statements of concern and the detail of measures it was taking to mitigate the situation.

NGOs are generally better placed and more active in raising issues, framing them and working in multiple arenas to promote their concerns. Some activist organisations are adept at moving issues to new arenas when they are losing in others. They often have less accountability than businesses, which allows them to make more questionable claims than companies can and internal structures that allow greater speed and flexibility in decision making.

While corporate issues management is often defensive it can be of significant benefit for companies or industries to create an issue and be the issues makers rather than simply responding to issues raised by others. Most readily available examples of constructively putting issues on the table can be found in the area of public policy. There have been campaigns by companies and business organisations who have taken the initiative to shape legislative priorities or challenge regulatory measures and to draw attention to industrial relations issues which affect productivity and national competitiveness, and to stimulate public demand for a local development.

ISSUES MANAGEMENT PROCESS

To facilitate strategic management of issues, a common framework has been adopted as a core process for corporate affairs departments. Some companies have developed this into complex systems and protocols and others have internalised the major concepts and proceed with less formal processes. The major steps in the issues management framework are:

- scan the environment to identify emerging issues, their convergence with social, economic and political trends and the potential influence of issues advocates,

- monitor these trends to assess potential impacts on the company or its mission to determine priorities,

- analyse the more significant of these issues to evaluate their potential impacts on the company and the company's capacity to influence outcomes,

- develop and implement plans and activities to respond to issues, and

- undertake post-hoc evaluation of outcomes to assist future planning.

SCANNING

One approach to the early identification of issues is the issues audit. Typically, this involves canvassing the views of major interest groups, media, regulators, academics, public servants, politicians and others with an interest in the company or industry, or who have the capacity to influence issues. A focus on issues in more general stakeholder audits is discussed in Chapter 5. The consultations explore what stakeholders see as emerging issues, and the capacity of the company to manage them. For frankness and objectivity, it is normal for an external consultant to conduct these audits. Experience has shown that stakeholders are frank with their opinions and appreciate companies making an effort to seek their views.

Other techniques such as surveys, opinion polling and focus groups can be used to identify and assess issues. Internal brainstorming involving various function specialisations and levels of seniority within the company is also commonly used. This is sometimes enhanced by the involvement of external participants to expose the company to outside perspectives.

Another approach to early identification has been the allocation of staff members to the task of monitoring issues in specific areas. One company appointed an emerging issues team of young, interested staff from the various specialisations and business units across the organisation. Their job was to scan allocated publications, electronic platforms and other sources of information, and pass on relevant information to a central point for collation. Under the guidance of the corporate affairs department, they met periodically to brainstorm and continuously reassess an emerging issues slate.

It is common for regular presentations on emerging issues to be made to a company's senior management team and board.

ASSESSING PRIORITIES

Major companies have hundreds of potential issues. Given resource constraints, it is important to focus on those most significant to the company. This requires an assessment of the potential impact of issues and the company's ability to influence their evolution and outcomes. It is common to represent this on a two-scale matrix.

ISSUE EVALUATION

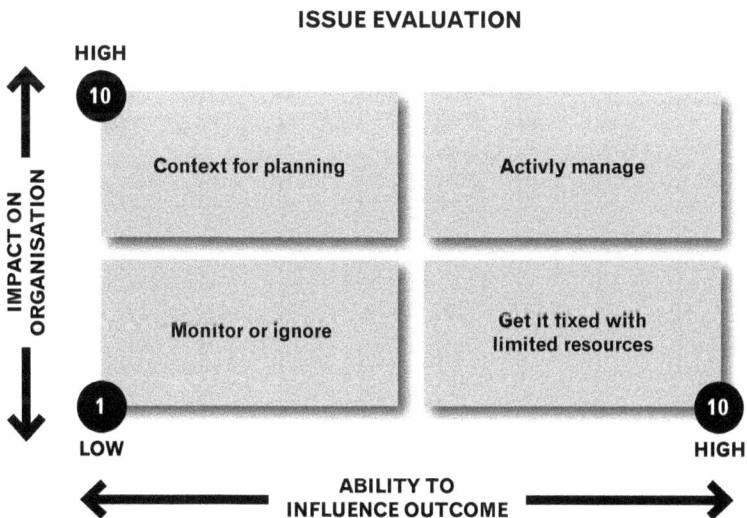

When an issue has a high potential impact and the company can influence the outcome, it should be actively managed with appropriate resources. However, if an issue has a high impact but is difficult to manage, a company should monitor the issue and take it into account in strategic planning. Many issues fall into this category such as cultural shifts like increased demands for gender equity, international trends like resistance to globalisation, or political shifts regarding emissions controls.

A company should not necessarily ignore an issue that has only a modest impact if it has a strong ability to influence it. It may be appropriate, based on a cost-benefit analysis, to take the limited action required to address it. Issues that currently do not warrant active management or appear low on the impact scale may nevertheless qualify as 'sleeper' candidates for periodic monitoring and assessment.

ISSUES MAPPING

This is a simple process of thinking about and pursuing a company's slate of issues. Some companies take a more structured approach to this than others. At the structured end of issues management, analysis is research-based and fully documented.

Mapping consists of an exposition of:

- the background: where the issue comes from and how it emerged,
- he players: who has an interest and how influential they might be,
- the arguments used as the issues unfold (this is important as addressing the arguments of issues advocates, rather than any unspecified but motivating interests, is unlikely to resolve conflict),
- the interests of the various players,
- the processes through which the issue might be played out,
- timeframes, including sequence of possible events to manage interventions strategically, and
- coalitions – positive and negative, existing and potential – with the capacity to move negative stakeholders to neutral and neutral stakeholders to supportive.

Based on this mapping, issues management strategies can be developed, but on some issues it can also lead to the modification of corporate plans to better align company objectives with political or other realities.

ISSUES DATABASES

At the most basic level, a database can simply be an electronic version of the traditional issues briefs that are designed to inform the management team of the status of an issue and the company's position in relation to it. A more comprehensive database might be developed, shared and maintained for the most important issues.

Issues strategies documented in a database need regular reviews to determine whether the current corporate responses remain appropriate or require deeper assessment and adjustment in terms of attention and resourcing. When widely shared and discussed, these processes can make management teams more sensitive to their external environment.

Management teams attest the value of these databases in improving the timeliness and cohesion of corporate responses to issues. Managers draw on them to assist in decision making; to pursue agendas in their industry associations; to incorporate details into stakeholder discussions and speeches; and to inform them during media interviews.

Example of an Issues Database

Major components of a database are:

- Issue: Identified by initial audit, contained in stakeholder impact statements or updated by corporate affairs staff in business unit.

- Potential impact: Nature and level of risk or opportunity.

- Stakeholder(s): Stakeholders who may be affected.

- Sensitivity: E.g. position is designated 'company in confidence', or unrestricted.

- Business owner: Most affected, accountable for the issue.
- Issues manager: Responsible corporate affairs executive.
- Issue team: (If appropriate) with relevant expertise.
- Spokesperson: Usually manager of the business unit most affected.
- Position paper status: Availability of a position statement.
- Stakeholder impact statement (SIS) status: Has SIS been prepared?
- Management plan: Including communications plan (required/available/not required?)
- Requirement to notify: Eg. stock exchange/government regulator.
- Expiry: 'Sunsetting' or review date/process.

Accessing the resources required to establish and maintain the most elaborate systems can be challenging. However, as noted, these systems can operate at a variety of levels of specificity from highly detailed for the most serious issues, to more broad-brush or less formal. Many companies have moved away from fully articulated systems due to the costs and complexities, but experience has shown that those who have been through the process at a reasonably articulated level have established a valuable issues management mindset. Those managers are more likely to apply the disciplines and structured processes instinctively.

PLANNING & EXECUTION

For critical issues, it may be appropriate to create an issue management team. These are normally led by the most senior line manager accountable for the issue (the issues owner) and someone responsible for driving the process and implementation, usually from the corporate affairs function (the issues manager). Participants should also include representatives of function specialisations relevant to the issue, for example legal, technical, and regulatory and external support.

The role of the issues management team is to develop a plan which includes specific goals, strategy and clear accountabilities for each relationship, task, or process. It should undertake periodic evaluation of progress and adjustment of the plan as required. Where issues are sufficiently significant, dedicated resources are often required for research or to lead communications activity, including taking executives 'off line' for all or parts of the task.

Effective plans will usually call on a multiplicity of public affairs tools beyond government relations and external communications. These may include enhanced knowledge management to maximise intelligence and coherence in the company's position, employee communications to enlist and maintain staff support and co–operation, and strategies for achieving community or stakeholder relations support.

One question in complex and decentralised companies is the location of responsibility for managing an issue. When should an issue be dealt with locally in a branch or geography, and when should it migrate to the corporate level? Issues can arise in a business unit without an adequate understanding of their broader implications for the company and, more commonly, a local issue can become a problem for the company as a whole.

To address this, organisations commonly centralise or at least coordinate issues management processes, including databases, with other mechanisms to enhance knowledge management and cohesion. The location and, if necessary, transfer of accountability for an issue can be managed through mutual agreement in a company-wide issues forum.

POST-HOC EVALUATION

The last phase of the formal process is to evaluate performance in managing the issue to inform future improvement. The questions that need to be asked include how well the issue was anticipated and understood; how quickly the company was able to respond; the effectiveness of the response; and what lessons can be learned.

CHAPTER FIVE: STAKEHOLDER MANAGEMENT

A stakeholder can be thought of as an individual or group who can affect or be affected by the actions, decisions, policies and practices or goals of the organisation.[22]

Stakeholder concepts in Western countries evolved over the past half century in parallel with the rise of participatory democracy – the demand for individuals or groups to have a direct say in matters that affect them.

As discussed in Chapter 8, the classical view of business is that the only goal of a company should be to maximise returns to shareholders – the rightful owners – by providing goods and services within the law and without fraud or deception. Responding to broader objectives is seen as a distraction from core business, diverting resources away from the owners and towards activities that are not the responsibility of the company.

As large public companies emerged in the latter part of the twentieth century the practical application of this classical model was questioned by management theorists who drew a distinction between owners (shareholders) whose resources are being used, and professional managers who had effective control of those resources. They cited General Motors as an example of this separation of ownership and control. Entrepreneurs who gave their names to Chevrolet, Oldsmobile, Packard and Buick initially had high degrees of individual control as well as ownership. Their companies merged to become General Motors and new shares were issued to a wide-ranging investment community. With the dilution and disaggregation of stockholding, owners ceased to be engaged in daily decisions and their roles became more like that of passive investors. Professional managers were perceived to act in their own interests in ways not always aligned with those of the owners of capital.

With the rise of social and political activism in the 1960s and 1970s, a third concept emerged. Attention was drawn to the impact of

22 Carroll AB & Buchholtz AK (1989) *Business and Society: Ethics and Stakeholder Management*, Cornell

companies on society, and large organisations were targeted as a cause of broad community harm. Companies were forced to realise that the expectations and demands of a wide range of actors could have a profound effect on their activities and performance. One theorist postulated a 'social environment model' based on:

> ... the explicit recognition that corporate behavior responds to political force, public opinion, and government pressures. Whereas both classical and managerial theory ignore the impacts of political forces, the social environment theory analyses corporate behavior as a response to both market and non-market forces because both affect the firm's costs, revenues and profits.[23]

The issue of stakeholder interests came into focus in a high-profile campaign by consumer activist Ralph Nader. At an annual general meeting of shareholders in May 1970, he and his supporters acquired a small amount of stock in General Motors and placed some proxy resolutions requiring certain actions by the company. While operating in the formal paradigm of shareholder rights, the campaign called for the appointment of an environmentalist, consumer advocate and minority leader to the board "who will insist that the board take into account the many social consequences of its decisions".[24]

Their proposals also sought to establish a committee that included unions, small shareholders and civil rights representatives to examine and report to shareholders and the public on the company's activities. While the campaign failed to win enough shareholder votes to command these outcomes, it generated widespread media attention and gained the support, for example, of church leaders, charitable foundations, pension funds and university foundations.

These ideas bled into the stakeholder theory of the firm, most prominently articulated by academic Ed Freeman in the 1980s. Without

23 Jacoby, NH (1974) 'The Corporation or Social Activist' in Prakash Sethi, (Ed) *The Unstable Ground: Corporate Social Policy in a Dynamic Society*, Melville Publishing

24 Campaign GM, Proxy Statement to Annual General Meeting of General Motors Corp. Detroit, 22 May, 1970

questioning the ultimate accountability of companies to shareholders, he championed the potential for mutual benefits, including for shareholders, from a constructive focus on other stakeholders who were impacted by a business and therefore had a legitimate claim on its actions.[25]

Professor Jennifer Griffin from the University of Chicago sees that serving stakeholder needs is enlightened self-interest, contributing to the hard-nosed interests of shareholders. She notes that while not all stakeholder demands or causes are appropriate or achievable, stakeholder action can lead to constructive innovation. A focus on stakeholder impact can provide management with a better understanding of the market and operating environment. It can improve products and services, identify issues early to reduce operational risk, and can build constructive coalitions on matters of mutual interest.

> *Forward-thinking business executives are interweaving impacts into everyday strategy decisions to co-create innovative, mutually beneficial value. By meeting the needs of core constituents and using unique resources and capabilities, the sweet spot of how value can be created is expanding.*[26]

Accordingly, engaging stakeholders and responding to their expectations is said to provide long-run return to shareholders.

Some modern versions of academic thinking in the US have, however, gone beyond the basic premise of the traditional theory of the firm and rationale of stakeholder responses as being in the interests of shareholders. They question the theoretical primacy of management accountability to the owners of capital.

> *The modern corporation is the center of a network of interdependent interests and constituents, each contributing (voluntarily or involuntarily) to its performance... Our proposed*

25 Freeman E (1984) *Strategic Management: A Stakeholder Approach*, Pitman, Boston

26 Griffin JJ (2016) *Managing Corporate Impacts: Co-Creating Value*, Cambridge University Press

redefinition of the corporation is based on this observation. Share-owners hold securities, but they do not own the corporation in any meaningful sense, nor are they the only constituents vital to its existence and success... [shareholder dominance] is inconsistent with the observed behaviour of successful firms. This leads the authors to place shareholders in line with other "stakeholders"... The corporation is an organisation engaged in mobilising resources for productive uses in order to create wealth and other benefits for its multiple constituents.[27]

Stakeholder interests frequently coalesce into pressure groupings. The owners of capital have institutional investors to bring pressure on management, as well as shareholder associations to lobby companies on their behalf. Employees have unions; suppliers have industry associations and the small business lobby; and many sectors and interests in the community come together to make demands of business in coalitions' organisations.

Starting with the chemical industry's code of conduct, developed in response to environmental and safety controversies in the 1980s, a requirement for stakeholder engagement is now enshrined in many industries' self-regulation codes. Many such codes oblige firms to regularly consult with community stakeholders and disclose data on environmental and other impacts on the community, under the threat of expulsion and loss of legitimacy in the marketplace. Commitment to stakeholder consultation is also often required of companies undertaking projects as a condition of regulatory approval.

Stakeholder relations can be seen as a competitive tool. Companies with intelligence about the attitudes and needs of stakeholders will be more effective in managing their concerns. Some companies have used engagement with stakeholders to more directly position themselves against competitors with subtle forms of 'push-polling' and other devices.

27   Post JE, Preston LE, Sachs S (2002) *Redefining the Corporation: Stakeholder Management and Organizational Wealth*, Stanford Business Books

Stakeholder expectations have also extended to the operations of government. Politicians and government agencies are obliged to routinely consult potentially impacted stakeholders ahead of making decisions, to maintain their legitimacy.

STAKEHOLDER MAPPING

Stakeholder management practice varies a lot between firms. It is common to categorise stakeholders in a variety of ways. For example, identifying whether they are internal or external to the organisation. Internal stakeholders might include shareholders, employees, management or various subdivisions of these. External stakeholders might be identified as primary (for example, those with a contractual relationship with the firm) or secondary, and then divided into various sub-categories.

Another approach is to categorise stakeholders in tiers as they are variously affected by or can affect the company. A stakeholder might move up a tier because of the potential impact of a particular decision taken by the company; the urgency of an issue; or the changing power of a stakeholder to impact the company. In determining a company strategy in relation to an issue, it is important to assess the level of its urgency or its salience for the stakeholder.

Savage et al depicts four stakeholder types.[28] Type 1 is high on potential cooperation, which suggests these stakeholders should be actively involved, possibly by seeking an alliance with them. Type 2 is low on both threat and potential for cooperation. The recommendation with this type is just to monitor and to act if the assessment changes. Type 3 is high on potential threat and low on cooperation, which suggests the need for a defensive strategy. And Type 4 is high on both potential for cooperation and threat, which requires active management and collaboration.

28   Savage GT., Nix, TH., Whitehead, CJ., Blair, JD., (1991) 'Strategies for Assessing and Managing Organizational Stakeholders' Administrative of Management Executive 5(2),

ENGAGEMENT PROCESSES

Managers need to decide the preferred nature and extent of engagement with stakeholders. In order to design strategies, allocate resources and optimise alignment with stakeholders, it is important to understand how they perceive the company is performing against their expectations, and how they would like to be informed or engaged.

A useful framework for identifying the appropriate degree of public engagement is Arnstein's 'Ladder of Citizen Participation'. This was first articulated in 1969, in relation to local government planning, but has been adopted to guide both government and business sector outreach.[29]

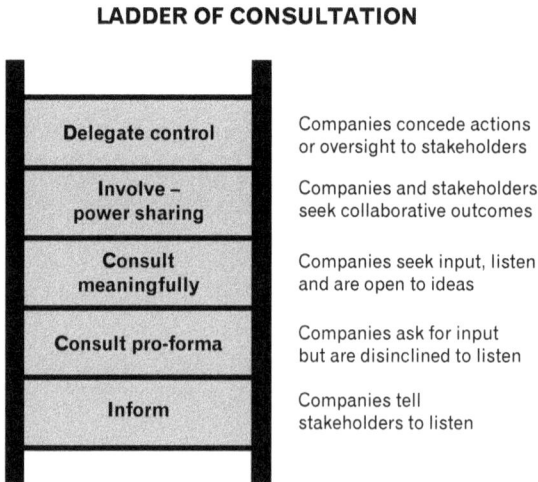

LADDER OF CONSULTATION

Delegate control	Companies concede actions or oversight to stakeholders
Involve – power sharing	Companies and stakeholders seek collaborative outcomes
Consult meaningfully	Companies seek input, listen and are open to ideas
Consult pro-forma	Companies ask for input but are disinclined to listen
Inform	Companies tell stakeholders to listen

The ladder depicts various levels of participation, from not informing and no participation at the base to ultimate delegation of decision-making power to stakeholders. The level of appropriate engagement is determined by circumstances and stakeholder expectations. At the low end of the ladder, companies operate without a mechanism for consultation or have limited capacity for feedback or stakeholder response to the company.

As stakeholders progress up the ladder, their participation becomes more meaningful, and they become more empowered. They

29   Arnstein, SR (July 1969) 'Ladder of Citizen Participation', *Journal of American Planning Association*, Vol 35 No4

are listened to with an increasing degree of attention and decision making is more deeply shared. Companies may be prepared to share decision making without pressure and can benefit from doing so. Full delegation to stakeholders is typically appropriate and is granted only when it is advantageous for achieving business goals. Examples include: a hamburger company ceding decisions on packaging to an environment group to protect its market with environmentally sensitive consumers; and a mining company ceding its management of affected woodlands to environmental activists in order to lift objections and win support for development approval.

In his advice to business, consultant and academic Pete Sandman sets out guidelines to accompany this ladder of communication and participation.[30] He says that stakeholders do not want or need to be consulted on everything, and when they are affected often just providing information will do. However, he suggests the management impulse to 'let sleeping dogs lie' is often the wrong call. There are often short-term benefits from not publicly highlighting issues but, in the long term, stakeholders expect open communication on issues that affect them. There are numerous examples of mangers underestimating stakeholder interest and concern. Where there is any doubt, Sandman says a company should elevate its approach to the next rung of the ladder. Where there is potential controversy, consultation can prevent outrage. When controversy exists, people will demand to provide input regardless. He notes that consultation and power sharing takes resources and time, but so does stakeholder hostility to company activities.

In addition to these considerations, it is important not to create expectations of outcomes that cannot or will not be fulfilled. It is also important to realise that stakeholders are not homogeneous and frequently do not agree among themselves about their interests or goals. Companies are often in the invidious position of having to balance the demands of disparate stakeholders while accommodating

30   Sandman, PM (1993) *Responding to Community Outrage: Strategies for Effective Risk Communication*, AIHA Press, Fairfax, Virginia

their own business needs. In many of these situations, governments at various levels are obliged to intervene to settle conflicts. A common example is competing stakeholder demands for conservation on one hand, and employment and regional development on the other.

To simply provide information is the most basic means of engaging stakeholders. This includes updates on websites and other online messaging, printed letterbox and media factsheets, and direct mail. For local developments, for example, media announcements, notice boards and mailouts to those potentially impacted are often mandated by government. This information can be accompanied by invitations to participate in an engagement process. However, there is often a poor response to generalised invitations to learn and be consulted, and this one-way communication does not provide a strong mechanism to understand community attitudes or to get the benefits of input and goodwill that could help achieve company objectives.

In one example, a company advertised in the local paper that its representatives would be in the city centre for several hours to provide information and address concerns about a proposed development near the town. When nobody turned up, they reported to head office that the community had no concerns, only to be surprised by local hostility when development began.

A more proactive example of consultation was a company seeking to establish a communications tower in a community that had a powerful advocacy group focused on the environment and visual amenity. Sensing potential resistance, the company, well ahead of the scheduled development, ran a campaign to explain the benefits of enhanced communication to leaders of emergency services, healthcare services and schools to demonstrate the contribution to convenience and personal safety of the proposed upgrade. As a result, the town's leadership easily overruled activist opposition and pushed for an accelerated timeframe.

A frequently used vehicle for stakeholder engagement is the community site visit. This not only provides an opportunity for direct contact but can be important to demystifying operations and developing trust. A variation is field visits, commonly provided to government actors, the media and organisations with a specific interest or concern. Stakeholder engagement to reduce concerns about risk is further discussed in Chapter 6.

Seeking to build relationships and trust with stakeholders through direct participation in corporate community investment is common. With or without corporate contributions, however, companies frequently encourage their executives and staff members to participate in community activities. This builds relationships but also helps staff understand community interests and concerns. Constructive relationships can also be built with activist stakeholders by working together in areas of common concern, even though they may be adversaries on some issues.

Advisory groups of stakeholders can operate at a variety of levels, even to boards of directors. They are most common however in local communities. The earliest major example of this journey up the ladder of engagement, and one that has been a model for companies subsequently, was the establishment, in 1989, of a community consultative committee for the Altona Petrochemical Complex in suburban Melbourne.

Community meetings, sometimes referred to as 'town halls', are common and can take a variety of forms. They can be initiated simply to disseminate information or help when issues have stirred up stakeholder concern. They provide an opportunity to dispel disinformation and demonstrate a willingness to listen and provide valuable feedback on community expectations and concerns. There are times when companies have no option but to call such meetings or to participate in town halls called by others.

Town halls need to be approached sensitively. These meetings can help to resolve issues but can also stoke opposition, as adversarial voices exploit the platform to enhance demands, build hostility and recruit others to their cause. The loudest voices may not be representative of broader stakeholder opinion but can distort the feedback companies may rely on in their decision making. High levels of diplomacy and political skill are often required to successfully chart the waters of town hall meetings.

Stakeholder surveys are common and can be undertaken by a variety of means, including online. Face-to-face third-party providers are most often used as intermediaries to conduct the surveys to optimise honesty in the expression of shareholder opinions. Surveys can serve as issues audits and are a core component of issues management systems.

Apart from providing immediate feedback, stakeholder databases that result from these surveys can capture key information about stakeholders and their interests to assist ongoing relationships. Surveys can also provide information relevant to communications strategies when respondents are asked about their sources of information and how and to what extent they would like to receive information from the company in the future.

It is often useful to report the findings of surveys back to stakeholders. This creates the opportunity to show their messages are being heard and taken seriously. It also enables a company to correct any disinformation and explain what it is doing to address any concerns.

Opinion polls assess views and attitudes on nominated topics by putting questions to a sample of a target-group population. They can provide a snapshot of current opinions but also plot trends in opinion over time. Design and sampling are critical. To be reliable, careful attention needs to be paid to the way questions are framed and the order in which they are asked. The size and representativeness of samples is also a critical factor in measuring opinion accurately.

Focus groups bring together small, representative collections of people from a target audience for facilitated but informal conversations on selected topics. Beyond eliciting opinions, they help gauge the reasons why positions are taken and allow for follow-up questions and non-verbal cues that provide a better understanding of relevant underlying emotions. They provide nuances not available through other means and shed light on issues and concerns that might otherwise be missed in surveys and questionnaires.

Practitioners and professional advisors these days are exploring

Altona's Community Consultation Committee

Altona's joint venture petrochemical companies had troubled relationships with local community members who were concerned about health issues arising from emissions. Initially the companies dismissed protests as a classic case of a 'not in my backyard' (NIMBY) protest.

However, after a period of serious conflict, the joint venture companies established an independent neighbourhood stakeholder group to discuss, monitor, and resolve issues at the Altona plant. Its stated goal was to: "Promote mutual understanding between local residents and the facility through improved plant performance and satisfactorily addressing residents' concerns." This required that the company cede some power but that was necessary to secure the community's and the government's acceptance of the plant's confirmed existence and future development.

The committee included resident and local government representatives, as well as the environment regulator, as observers. Minutes were published and anyone was invited to attend and participate in discussions. The company's acceptance of the community's 'right-to-know' expectations led to full disclosure of their development plans (except for information covered by strict commercial-in-confidence criteria) and the committee's proceedings were openly reported in the local press.

Within five years, the community group had, with company support, established environment monitoring teams with a 24-hour hotline to the plant to provide feedback on vagrant emissions. Odours that did not originate from the plant were identified by community leaders. Issues were raised directly with the companies and, where possible, resolved by the plant rather than by regulators. This gave community members a feeling of greater control. Trust was also built with environment and safety regulators who, satisfied with the effectiveness of these arrangements, moved from detailed 'tap and tick' environmental monitoring to more flexible, co-regulatory provisions.

sophisticated data analytics and are following political strategists and marketing specialists into the opportunities of new technologies. In addition to highly developed models for reputation measurement and insight using traditional quantitative and qualitative research methods, many corporate affairs functions are also investing in technology and specialist staff to enable their strategies to be more data driven.[31]

These investments reflect the massive societal shift to digital and social media over recent decades and the ability to use data from these sources to listen to stakeholders at both macro and micro levels. This targeted data has the advantage of being derived in real-time and at lower cost. It provides organisations with a rich stream of strategic and tactical information to measure and improve communications effectiveness and to strengthen engagement with a diverse array of stakeholders and the wider community.

---

31 Page Society Report (2019) 'The CCO as Pacesetter', knowledge.page.org/report/the-cco-as-pacesetter

CHAPTER SIX: RISK COMMUNICATION & CRISIS MANAGEMENT

Around 70% of major companies will have a crisis of some sort over a five-year period, according to studies. Some issues are managed effectively, and some poorly, with lasting negative consequences for the company and often for their industry. Some sectors are more prone to crises than others, but none are exempt. Approaches to dealing with risk and preparing for crises are now widely adopted but execution is still often wanting.

Wayne Burns, Executive Director, Centre for Corporate Public Affairs

Corporate affairs departments have a key role in risk assessment, risk mitigation, risk communication and crisis management. The concepts, techniques and skills of corporate affairs personnel are central to the successful operation of risk and crisis management.

RISK COMMUNICATION

The intuitive approach of business managers trained in science or economics is to use scientific and economic data to assess statistical probabilities and to calculate the trade-off between risk and long-term gains. This is not necessarily the same frame through which stakeholders view the risks, and presenting data is rarely effective when attempting to appease concerns.

Firms have turned to experts to support them in assuaging community concerns, but populist advocates have at times inoculated citizens against ready acceptance of this expertise.[31]

Economic and scientific modelling rarely satisfies the protective parent worried about overhead transmission lines or the effect of a product substance or plant emission on a child's development. Science makes little difference when people feel frightened, powerless or suspicious that they are being conned. Nor does more scientific data deter the dramatic story-seeking journalist or politician motivated to exploit a controversy.

It is natural for managers, feeling frustrated by what they perceive to be irrational, to respond with hostility or negative stereotyping of opponents. But when reassuring people, it is unhelpful to suggest that they are stupid or malevolent. An influential book[32] and subsequent writings of academic and consultant Peter Sandman has contributed

31   Bell S, Hindmoor A & Umashev N (2013) 'The Determinants of Corporate Political Activity in Australia', *Australian Journal of Political Science* p.12

32   Sandman PM (1993) *Responding to Community Outrage: Strategies for Effective Risk Communication*, AHIA Press

to businesses' understanding of risk communication. He says the term 'risk' has two components, with important distinctions between them. He calls 'hazards' those things that are likely to cause harm. They reflect how bad a problem might be, multiplied by the probability of it happening. The other component, which he calls 'outrage', refers to how upset people are.

Accordingly, the idea of risk for the purposes of risk communication can be reduced to the formula: Risk=Hazard+Outrage. A company's risk communication, therefore, should be employed to enhance concern when the hazard is high but concern is low. For example, stakeholders can be apathetic on issues like safety in the workplace, conservation, climate change, smoking or dietary health risks where there is real hazard and it is important to raise awareness. There are many situations in which companies have both an interest and a moral duty to mitigate apathy and stress the risks.

However, when the hazard is low but the outrage is high, risk communication should be used to lower concerns. Examples of low or imperceptible risk but high concern and outrage are common in relation to such issues as food additives, vaccinations, windfarms or benign plant emissions in local neighbourhoods.

Outrage can be enhanced by activists who seek to put pressure on companies by promoting the perception of hazards (with the media providing a ready megaphone for those who voice concerns). It is only when outrage is mitigated and calm is established that economic and scientific arguments can be heard and understood.

Sandman offers a list of human factors that facilitate outrage and that need to be considered when developing risk communication strategies.[33] He notes that people are more prone to be outraged by things that are coerced or involuntary, rather than what they are in control of. He uses the example of the differences between voluntarily skiing down a snow-covered hill and being "pushed down on a pair of sticks".[34] People like to feel comfortable and in control, especially

33 Sandman PM (Nov 1987) 'Risk Communication: Facing Public Outrage' *EPA Journal* p 21–22

34 Sandman PM (Nov 1987) 'Risk Communication: Facing Public Outrage' *EPA Journal* p 21–22

regarding the management of something they perceive to be a risk. A lack of control can create resentment as well as fear, and both factors lead to outrage.

Executives seeking to develop a strategy for managing stakeholder outrage find it counterintuitive to relinquish control and to involve external stakeholders in decision making. Nevertheless, there are times when it is appropriate to enable outsiders to have, and to feel they have, influence over the issues they perceive to be hazards. As discussed in Chapter 5, the establishment of informed community advisory councils with influence can help the community to understand hazards and ease concerns.

Where trust is established and community relations are strong, it is not unusual for communication hotlines to be connected to a plant's control room. In one neighbourhood in the US, for example, senior citizens are trained as 'odour sniffers' who can tell their neighbours what is going on in the atmosphere and can contact the company to report the problem where necessary. As a monitoring resource for the company, they became a trusted source of information for their peers, able to manage rumours and disinformation to calm any unnecessary fears and consequent outrage. Community members feel they have more control. It is said: "There is not much comfort when the company or industry is the fox who tells us not to worry because the hen house is safe. We need to hear the chickens say that."

Being open to stakeholder involvement in decision making does not necessarily mean surrendering to pressure. Proposed solutions offered by stakeholders may not pass a cost-to-benefit test and may not be technically or in other ways viable. Similarly, the demands of one stakeholder group often conflict with those of another. However, active listening, and sometimes responding by sharing control when the situation demands it, are viable strategies for dealing with outrage and facilitating the task of management.

In one example, a community valued the economic contributions of a gold mining operation to the local area but were concerned about the potential toxicity of a tailings dam and agitated to have it removed. The company responded by telling the community to trust them because they had done the research and there was no reason to worry. However, pressure built until the company was forced to switch tack and open its books. The community observed the company's total environment control program and came to understand that while the tailings dam was one of the company's challenges, it would cost a much larger proportion of the environment mitigation budget than higher-order priorities to fix. After seeing the whole picture for themselves, the citizens supported the company's approach.

Linked to the issue of control is Sandman's suggestion that people are also more fearful and prone to protest about issues that are exotic rather than familiar, and industrial rather than natural. The use of technical and scientific jargon is a case in point. One might find it scary to ingest ethyl methylphenylglycidate but this is just the chemical formula of strawberry flavouring. For this reason, advertisers always stress the natural ingredients in food products or cosmetics. Similarly, community neighbours can be disturbed by pipes and gas emissions emanating from behind the high walls and Hazchem signs at a petrochemical plant, so plant managers are encouraged to host open days to make their operations more familiar and approachable.

Another factor that is likely to enhance concern and drive outrage is the unknowable. Risk, by definition, implies uncertainty and the possibility of unintended consequences. For example, the negative impact of pharmaceuticals on patients can be difficult to quantify. Some people have a greater tolerance for risk than others, but it is natural to desire confidence and certainty. It would be easy to mitigate concern if a trusted manager with credibility was able to say there was zero risk around issues of concern, but there is rarely zero risk and to assert it would be misleading or even illegal.

Being seen as unresponsive or lacking in empathy about issues that concern stakeholders can also be a factor that exacerbates outrage. A potent cause of community outrage is the perception that the interests of community members have not been considered in decisions that affect them. Trust, on the other hand, is built when stakeholders believe an organisation is conscious of their concerns and sensitive to them.

The track record of a company will also have an impact on the

Employees Speak Out

A North American nuclear plant was under attack from an anti-nuclear activist group. The group organised protest meetings and demonstrations, and waged a campaign on social media. Its claims about processes at the plant and safety concerns for employees and the neighbourhood stirred up insecurity and concern in the surrounding community. After a series of hostile 'town hall' meetings organised by protestors, staff at all levels of the plant felt the situation was being misrepresented and volunteered to speak out in support of the company. With approval from management, they became active in social media where they shared their knowledge, experience and opinions. In doing so, they were able to actively rebut exaggeration and misinformation. They also volunteered to speak on behalf of the company in paid local print and television commercials. Because they were well informed and had much at stake themselves, the staff were perceived to be more credible than the company hierarchy, and their messages helped to mitigate the community's concerns.

way messages about risk are accepted. If a company has a history of misleading stakeholders, or has a poor reputation in general, its messages can be met with skepticism, making assuaging concerns more difficult. Companies with better reputations have more credibility and they are more likely to get the benefit of the doubt when issues arise. Winning that trust might involve acknowledging past bad behavior and accepting blame. Trust is built when a company is perceived as honest about the level of hazard related to its operations and information about risk is openly shared.

In many circumstances it has been useful to involve employees in communications about risk. Companies and government agencies have traditionally been reluctant to let employees speak out on controversies confronting their organisation, yet employees often have special credibility in these situations. They are an important informal source of external opinion in relation to their organisation, and it is important that they are kept fully aware of the issues and circumstances. In many cases, employees and their families live in the communities that perceive the risk and the fact that they too would be affected by any negative impacts adds credibility.

Of course, in many cases employees themselves may be a key stakeholder group for risk communications and assurance, both because of their own concerns and because they often bear the brunt of community outrage against the company they work for. Negative impressions arise and mitigation opportunities are missed if employees admit they have not been informed or that they are not allowed to talk about the issues causing concern.

RISK & CRISIS MANAGEMENT

Crises are situations or events that have the potential to seriously damage a company. They can arise at any time and without warning. They can be a system failure, financial collapse, product defect or contamination, illegal activity such as fraud, fire, safety issue or environmental damage. A crisis can also be a result of ethical failures, such as human rights issues or unacceptable workplace behaviour. They can be unpredictable and outside the control of management, such as a natural disaster, or can evolve from a failure of technical management or corporate culture.

The negative impacts on a firm of a crisis, including financial cost and loss of reputational capital, are often significantly enhanced by poor management responses. Perceived failure to address a crisis promptly, slow or clumsy communications, even inappropriate body language, can seriously exacerbate damage. There are numerous examples when the poor management of an event or issue has had a significantly greater negative impact than the issue itself.

Accordingly, companies of any scale should have risk management plans that anticipate crises and guide management. These plans are important in ensuring companies are as well prepared as possible, and to prevent counterproductive knee-jerk reactions by executives under pressure. Overseeing these systems is an important responsibility of CEOs and boards.

Systems and processes vary greatly between companies, but they have several elements in common. The first part of a plan is risk assessment. Risk-assessment processes are common across most management and technical functions of the modern corporation.

Risk assessment should include socio-political risk and be informed by issues management systems that recognise triggers that could escalate an issue into a crisis. The system should identify what could go wrong and have an impact on the company or its stakeholders, and must also evaluate, through risk rating, the likelihood of those risks occurring and their potential impact. These risk-assessment processes cannot guarantee that all risks can be anticipated and their impact successfully evaluated, but they do help to prioritise potential issues for attention and the application of resources.

ISSUE EVALUATION

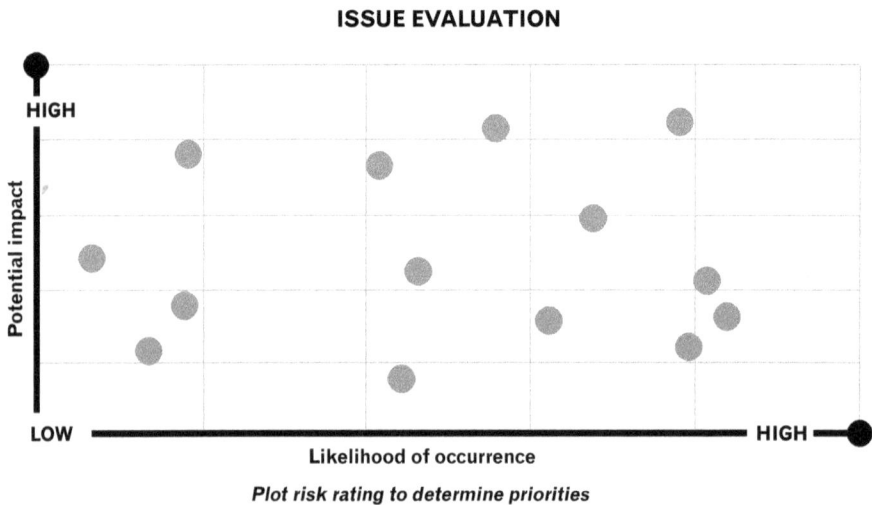

Plot risk rating to determine priorities

Having identified the nature and level of risk, registers are constructed and regularly reviewed. They prioritise risks for attention and, where possible, identify risk mitigation strategies.

It is important to establish clear accountabilities. Risk 'owners' are normally the executives whose business is likely to be most impacted by the crisis. Risk 'managers' are usually the corporate affairs executives responsible for handling communications and other non-operational

RISK REGISTER

RISK DESCRIPTION	RISK RATING	RISK OWNER	RISK MANAGER	MITIGATION STRATEGY

responses. Some large and vulnerable companies also have dedicated risk management teams.

While much will be unknowable, crisis management plans can be developed for broad categories of risk, such as operational risk, reputational risk, personnel risk and financial risk, to prepare for various contingencies. Within each, there can be several sub-categories, for example: plant explosions, oil spills, food contamination, computer glitches or executive scandals. Considering broad types of crises before they arise allows for a quick and efficient response. Most importantly, broad-based contingency plans can help a company to rapidly stem a crisis and potentially save lives, property, costs and reputation.

Key components of risk management plans include identifying potential stakeholders, essential services organisations whose support might be needed, and the legal and regulatory issues that might be involved.

The first element of any crisis plan is to fix the problem as quickly and effectively as possible. It is important to equip those responsible for sorting out technical and like problems, to do their job of minimising harm while seeking business continuity without distraction. However, effective management also requires speed in providing public information about a crisis. These two areas of focus – operational and communications – need to be closely coordinated.

At the outset, of course is the need to share 'instructing information' to let victims or potential victims know what to do to protect themselves and others. It is then critical to disseminate 'adjusting information' to communicate what the company is doing to prevent the crisis from reoccurring, to give the audience information on reparation efforts, and to convey messages of concern or sympathy towards the affected parties.[35]

---

35 Coombs TW (2010) 'Protecting Organization Reputations During a Crisis: The Development and Application of Situational Crisis Communication Theory', *Corporate Reputation Review*

Quick and effective instructing information is also in the interests of the company to preserve reputation, mitigate operational impacts and limit the need for compensation and potential legal costs. Where relevant, governments and regulators insist on receiving the earliest possible information and listed companies also need to manage the requirement to notify the stock exchange before the public of any crisis that is 'material'.

It is important that the company becomes the primary and trusted source of information with the general public and key stakeholders. The company should seek to control the narrative so as to prevent rumours, deal with disinformation, and prevent activists from inappropriately exploiting a crisis.

When facts are unknown or uncertain, it still important to go public with holding statements to explain the state of knowledge whilst committing to provide further information as it comes to hand. It is important not to speculate or deliberately underestimate the situation as subsequent contrary information will create distrust and expose a company that is not in control. In one widely reported case of nationwide telecommunications failure, confusion and a loss of confidence was caused by premature, and subsequently contradicted, speculations by the company on the cause and the extent of the problem. This confusion allowed others to step in and control the narrative. The way the crisis was managed, rather than the crisis itself, led to a customer revolt and the resignation of the CEO. This is just one of many cases in which the response to an issue created more damage than the issue itself.

Preparing draft templates and messages with open elements to be later filled in with emerging details, and getting legal clearance for those templates, enables public statements and communications with key stakeholders, including regulatory authorities, to be enacted as quickly as possible. The plan should be regularly updated with contact information for the most relevant people or groups. A hierarchy of priority for the receipt of information should also be established and documented.

Pre-crisis preparation should also include plans for the establishment of cross-functional crisis management teams for various categories of serious risk. Normally these teams would be led by the manager (issues owner) whose responsibilities are directly related the issue. Operations, legal, human resources and, where appropriate, marketing, along with corporate affairs should be part of the team. Depending on the nature of the crisis, some companies also include industrial relations and community liaison staff and sometimes even unions and external insurance representatives. Without letting it interfere with recovery, operations managers involved in the crisis need to be involved in any strategy discussions.

As with risk assessment processes, it is important to allocate clear responsibilities and accountabilities. Corporate affairs has the significant role of organising and coordinating the company's communications response and relationships with external stakeholders. Consistency is enhanced by the designation of a spokesperson or spokespeople and ensuring there is only one company message. The spokesperson will normally be the head of the relevant operation or a corporate affairs executive. The public will also reasonably expect the CEO to front the media as early as possible and take responsibility. On several significant occasions, the reluctance of a CEO to front up quickly after a crisis added to the scale of the problem. When a group of miners were caught underground for a week with an uncertain future, the complex ownership structure of the operation left a vacuum of leadership and responsibility and no obvious spokesperson. For the whole week, union leaders, with their own agenda, filled the vacuum and controlled the narrative and framing of the issue.

It is important to be as cooperative and helpful with the media as possible. The availability of background information on the company, infographics, photos and film, and any other helpful material, will facilitate quick and useful reporting and consolidate the company as the go-to and authoritative source of information. When there are industrial accidents or environmental problems, it might be tempting to shield the media from unpalatable locations. Experience has shown however that if the media is not taken by the company to see the problem firsthand, they will find their own way, with outcomes that may be worse.

Tone and body language are important and, regardless of the circumstances, a company in crisis needs to show regret and empathy for affected people. It is a bad look for a CEO to roll into a suffering community in an executive jet, or to complain about the inconvenience for the company or its personnel.

It is a natural human instinct when under pressure to find excuses or justifications, to diminish problems, to attack accusers or find other people or things to blame. Managers are no exception. However, lawyers and insurance companies will be wary of the precise language used by companies, as litigants can interpret expressions of regret as admissions of guilt where guilt may not be appropriately ascribed.

Drills, or crisis simulations, are a key element in preparation for a crisis and should be undertaken at least once a year, particularly when there is a high turnover of staff. Regular drills help to streamline responses and identify problems in plans and the allocation of responsibilities. Drills should involve crisis teams, other staff who will need to play a role if a crisis emerges and, where appropriate, the relevant externals such as the emergency services providers.

In one high-profile legal case it was revealed that the company had abandoned drills. They had sophisticated manuals and protocols for dealing with emergencies but when liability for a major plant disaster was being determined, the court found the manuals had not been read, leading to a slow and confused response.

Post-crisis strategies are also important. Strong positive relationships with stakeholders can build political capital, which gives a company the benefit of the doubt when situations arise.

The most effective strategy for salvaging reputation has been called 'mortification', a genuine expression of sorrow and regret for victims of a crisis. This of course needs to be authentic and needs to be perceived as such. Demonstrations of concern help to shift the emphasis from guilt to repairing damage, helping victims, and working aggressively to rectify the cause of the crisis.

Some companies compound their problems when they try to minimise the loss of reputational capital by throwing blame elsewhere. Others resist compensating victims or offer compensation that is considered inadequate or mean. The offer of limited compensation by an airline following a major business interruption and cancelled flights triggered a consumer revolt that amounted to a second-round crisis.

The discussion of legal strategies in Chapter 12 is relevant to the management of crises. A balance needs to be struck in some instances between winning legal arguments and losing reputational capital. Companies need to be conscious of this when being advised by external counsel focused on the black-letter law, and by insurance companies who have little reputational stake but significant financial stake in legal outcomes.

Positive Relationships

Companies will be better tolerated, recover faster, and be damaged less if they have a strong reputation and no history of crises. A positive example relates to an oil spill at a company facility on a harbour near middle-class private housing. The company had done such a good job in maintaining positive neighbourhood relations that the media could not get residents or political leaders to criticise it. In another example, cited in Chapter 5, after a huge chemical fire, a neighbourhood protected the company against activists because they trusted it. On the other hand, politicians will enhance their political capital by criticising a company if it is not in good standing with its community and defend a company if it is.

CHAPTER SEVEN: INTEREST GROUPS & THE DYNAMICS OF ADVOCACY

The non-market environment is populated by hundreds of activist groups, although some of them have only brief periods of activity. Because these groups shape the non-market environment of business and the non-market agendas of individual firms, managers must be aware of their organisation, agenda and tactics.

Lawrence Rothenberg, Professor of Political Science, University of Rochester

An important role in corporate affairs is to monitor, understand and respond to the activities of non-government interest groups and activists who seek to influence the socio-political environment of their company.

They can be defined in a variety of ways but, for our purposes, they are any group that is aggregated to pursue an idea or interest. Their nature and objectives are very diverse. They can be conservative or radical, can pursue a broad interest or be focused narrowly on a single issue. They can be permanent or transitory, forming and reforming as issues arise and evolve. They can operate at the grassroots level reflecting a broad general coalition, or represent the elite, made up of experts and leaders in their various communities. Their motives can be open and public spirited, or reflect narrow self-interest masquerading as concern for the public interest. Churches, trade unions, groups of neighbours concerned about housing redevelopments, or even business organisations and professional associations, can all be considered interest groups as they pursue their causes and policies.

Interest groups and activists play an important role in society by bringing attention to issues that need to be addressed, and giving voice to those who would otherwise be voiceless. Companies can also be better off when interest groups alert them to issues that may need to be addressed and, if not responded to early, may incur greater cost in the future.

On the other hand, interest group pressure can lead to outcomes that are sub-optimal or have negative impacts on companies and communities. While some interest groups are collaborative and seek to find win-win solutions, those with absolutist tendencies see cooperation and compromise with business as weakness. Their approach can be doctrinaire and disinterested in finding workable solutions ahead of achieving their full objectives.

Interest groups seek to influence the behaviour of business by applying economic pressure directly on companies. Some strategies include: seeking to pressure business through an increase in costs, for example advocating deterrent taxation; and pushing governments and regulators to mandate behaviour. Interest groups understand the value of reputation on the social licence to operate, and on the value of brands, and are quick to exploit these vulnerabilities.

The weapon of boycott is applied in a variety of forms. Consumers are asked not to purchase goods or services from the target company or industry. Common examples of boycotts occur when activists are concerned with human rights issues in the supply chain or products that may harm the environment. Other forms of boycott occur when unions withdraw labour to pressure companies, or when industries threaten the government with capital strikes.

Secondary boycotts are applied when a supplier is under pressure to deny goods or finance to a company. Examples include pressure placed on banks not to finance certain resource or energy developments for environmental reasons, and on media companies not to advertise a company's products.

Direct action, for example interrupting forest clearing or standing in the way of trucks entering a warehouse, is another is form of boycott.

Interest groups also employ legal strategies to change corporate behaviour. Legal action does not always have to be successful in court to achieve objectives. It causes costs and delays, and by bringing attention to issues, inflicts reputational damage regardless of the action's legal merit. Interest group plaintiffs have shown less constraint in generating media attention to issues involved in litigation than companies advised by conservative lawyers with their focus on black-letter law.

Some campaigns go to the heart of company governance with attempts to enlist shareholder support. Activists seek to highlight their causes by pressuring institutional investors and through shareholder resolutions at annual general meetings. Some also pressure companies to resign from industry associations that are leading the fight against their agenda. These are all forms of secondary boycott.

Interest groups are adept at building coalitions of interests to strengthen their campaigns. One high profile example was the attempt of unions in an industrial campaign to mount global pressure on a company by invoking a range of environment and human rights issues. Disguising their underlying industrial objective in the process, unions were able to enlist leaders of a wide range of interest group organisations and their issues to put pressure on the company.

Activist organisations have increasingly sought to back their claims with economic and scientific research. By the turn of the century, activists were supplementing declamatory rhetoric and stunts with solid research and evidence. While some of this is undertaken within well-resourced interest groups, it is more frequently undertaken in collaboration with academics or within sympathetic think tanks. Groups of scientists or economists with common concerns, such as climate change or international trade, can themselves adopt the mantle of interest groups as they push their agendas. It is not hard to find a scientist or economist who will support a cause. Sophisticated debate between contending parties takes place on the validity of methodologies and their findings and their implications for society and public policy.

Most of these advocacy strategies are mediated through the media to influence public opinion and create pressure for political or regulatory change. Interest group advocates are often well resourced and skilled at producing articles and media appearances, and can sometimes initiate and collaborate in investigative journalism. The media appetite for stunts, demonstrations and quarrels promotes attention given to activities and causes. The newsworthiness of conflict encourages polarisation and results in a decline of nuance in arguments.

Social media, now the main source of information for many in the community, has provided a variety of tools for interest groups to win influence and push causes. Barriers to entry are low for less well-resourced activists, making it easier and faster for activists to mobilise. Social media facilitates the use of celebrities and influencers to endorse the positions of activists. Meanwhile, loose rules about distortion and disinformation on social media work to the disadvantage of more staid businesses and governments who are more accountable and consequently constrained.

Interest groups are often able to exert influence when they are included in decision-making structures. This ensures the perspectives of the various parties are better understood and incorporated into consensual solutions. The most obvious examples are government advisory councils, reference panels or direct involvement in regulatory agencies, and participation in corporate stakeholder advisory councils or groups.

Not infrequently, however, the issue of 'representativeness' of advocates for a particular interest or the community is controversial. Those who identify themselves, or are seen by others, as proxies for consumers, taxpayers, public transport or even neighbourhood representatives, for example, may not always accurately reflect the positions of their claimed constituents. Differences in objectives, priorities and strategies can abound within categories of interest, leading to competing claims on business and government. This is apparent, for example in the environment movement, between those most concerned about climate change and those who see nuclear power as a partial solution, or those in communities with the competing priorities of employment and environmental protection. The high visibility and 'noisiness' of activists can also distort the level of importance a community attaches to it.

DYNAMICS OF ADVOCACY

Several factors mitigate constructive engagement with issues adversaries and make it difficult for issues to be resolved with dispassionate and objective analysis. Advocates on all sides are rewarded politically for reducing complex or nuanced issues to black-and-white propositions.

Issues adversaries – both interest groups and corporate executives – are prone to negatively stereotyping their opponents by attributing to them false motives and creating a 'straw man'. The straw man technique of argument is the erection of a false or exaggerated claim for the position an adversary is taking, and then attacking them on the grounds of this false representation.

An ever-present element in the dynamics of advocacy is the

natural tendency to rationalise a vested interest as a more generalised good. People motivated by their own interests often, consciously or subconsciously, corral the high moral ground of rights, entitlements and the public interest to support them. For example, public good is invariably cited as the motive for so-called NIMBY (not-in-my-backyard) campaigns rather than the preservation of amenity or property values. Public interest, rather than company or shareholder interest, is invariably cited in the advocacy campaigns of business.

Another inhibitor to the resolution of issues between companies and interest groups is occupational or issue myopia. This is the tendency to overweight the significance of issues people are professionally committed to or most fully involved in. Artists may ascribe higher than average value to the aesthetic, business leaders to economic efficiency, environmentalists to the state of nature, scientists to research, and so on. This gives rise to assumptions that others should prioritise their areas of concern in the same way. Many are unable or unprepared to see the need for governments and businesses to balance their demands with other worthy priorities.

Ambit claiming is a common process in which individual sectors or interests stake a claim for decisions or resources, exaggerating them to maximise their position in inevitable trade-offs or compromises as solutions are sought. A serious consequence of the constant assertion of a case is the tendency for advocates to ultimately believe in the ambit position taken, leading them to further solidify their positions and deepen their resolve. Constant assertion of a position, and the denial of validity of alternatives, tends to lock an advocate into the proposition they are making, further limiting their capacity to see alternative perspectives.

For the most radical groups, confrontation is the preferred or only option. Activist Saul Alinsky was an influential teacher of tactics to radical activists in the 1960s. His focus was on how communities of interest can take on governments and corporations. Some activists still apply his strategies and tactics today. He set out several characteristics of a good activist. First, a good activist should be irreverent, stirring unrest by insulting, agitating and discrediting. Having a sense of humour is required, "for the most important weapons for mankind are satire and ridicule".[36] He says a good activist knows there can be no action until an issue is totally polarised. Success only comes when followers believe "their cause is 100% on the side of the angels and that the opposition is 100% on the side of the devil".[37]

BUSINESS STRATEGIES

Alinsky suggests: "The real action is the enemy's reaction." He sees radical strategies benefiting from the intuitively hostile response to activist attacks on the part of companies. Corporate executive responses can often be driven by outrage without careful consideration. Responses may need to be strong but should be carefully calibrated.

Corporate affairs executives need to consider a number of dynamics at play when guiding their companies through engagement with interest group and issue adversaries. Many of these – such as respectful listening, building relationships, and being transparent to build trust – are discussed in Chapter 5 on stakeholder engagement.

The mining industry in Australia went through a steep learning curve on the dynamics of advocacy in the 1990s. In previous decades, a significant gap opened up between community expectations and mining industry behaviour, particularly related to the environment and Indigenous ownership of land.

The industry placed itself in stubborn opposition to changing expectations. It mistakenly thought that technical data on the environment and studies of economic benefits of the industry were adequate responses to rising criticism. Beyond that, its public advocacy was heavy-handed and insensitive. Politicians reflected on the deteriorating public image, one declaring, "When I need a leg-up in my electorate, I get stuck into the [mining] industry; it works every time." The stridency of its campaigns caused industry

36   Alinsky SD (1971) *Rules for Radicals: A Pragmatic Primer for Realistic Radicals*, Random House, NY

37   Alinsky SD (1971) *Rules for Radicals: A Pragmatic Primer for Realistic Radicals*, Random House, NY

Saul Alinsky's Rules for Radicals

- **Power is not only what you have but what your enemy thinks you have.**
  He elaborates with an analogy using the features of a face. The eyes: if you have organised a vast, mass-based people's organisation you can parade it visibly before the enemy and openly show your power. The ears: if your organisation is small in numbers, do what biblical Gideon did, conceal the numbers in the dark but raise enough din and clamour to make the audience believe your organisation is much larger. The nose: if your organisation is too tiny to make a noise, stink it
  up a bit.

- **Never go outside the experience of your people.**
  To do so creates confusion, fear and retreat.

- **Wherever possible, go outside the experience of your enemy.**
  Cause confusion, fear and retreat by not allowing them to fight on familiar territory.

- **Make the enemy live up to their book of rules.**
  It can be extremely difficult to always live up to one's aspirations and a great embarrassment when you are publicly found wanting. For example, it's hard for Christians to always adhere to the strict moral tenants of Christianity.

- **Ridicule is man's most potent weapon.**
  It is difficult to counteract ridicule. It infuriates the opposition who then react to your advantage.

- **A good tactic is one you enjoy.**
  If you are not having fun, something is wrong with the tactic.

- **A tactic that drags on too long is a drag.**
  Protestors get bored and drift off.

- **Keep the pressure on.**
  Be unrelenting with every opportunity and vehicle at your disposal. Pressure generates reactions that are essential to success. Properly goaded and guided, your enemy's reaction can be your major strength.

- **The price of a successful attack is a constructive alternative.**
  You cannot risk being trapped by the enemy by his sudden agreement with your demand – asking you what to do with this issue.

- **Pick the target, freeze it, personalise it and polarise it.**
  Given the capacity of governments or companies to shift responsibility, it is necessary to pick out someone to blame. You need a specific target on which to centre attacks. When responsibility is diffused or distributed, attack becomes impossible. One only acts decisively in the conviction that all the angels are on one side and all the devils are on the other.

representatives to lose their influence, while stakeholders in other sectors, including pastoralists, were able to negotiate on relevant issues with government.

Finally acknowledging failure, the mining industry association commissioned and accepted a consultants' report, which recommended the industry should be more empathetic and engage more openly with its critics. It recommended improved self-regulation through best-practice commitments and a stronger code of conduct. Also, it proposed the industry should be more constructive in public policy and seek closer alignment with the broader imperatives of government and engage more openly with their adversaries. As many of the mining industry's major issues are global, the report proposed that greater leadership be taken on engagement with international critics.

A series of speeches by the industry's most respected leaders carried this message forward, resulting in changes to both behaviour and attitudes. While behaviour was not uniform, and trust with the community not fully restored, the industry worked to build trusted, co-operative relationships with industry detractors. When the government announced a mining super-profits tax initiative during a boom in commodity prices, the industry received support from unions and environmentalists, and public sentiment forced the government to back down. This would not have been possible without a change in the general approach of the industry to dealing with its critics.

Research following a period of hostility between environment groups and timber companies showed that where personal relationships were established – regardless of differences in views – there was more trust, and less negative stereotyping or attribution of an insidious motive. It demonstrated that familiarity between managers and activists based in well-constructed consultation, and even better, social interaction, reduces distrust and facilitates better understanding between contending parties. (For this reason, the more strident activist organisations that seek to maintain conflict and resist compromise discourage direct relationships with their issues adversaries.[38])To improve relationships and build trust, it is now common for companies and industry associations to establish joint projects with advocacy organisations on issues of common interest, to involve them in advisory mechanisms and even, in some cases, to delegate power for the management of selected activities. These approaches are discussed further in Chapter 5.

Another impediment to the constructive resolution of issues can be termed the 'divorce lawyer syndrome.' This occurs when third

---

38   Hancock, P (1993) *Green & Gold: Sustaining Mineral Wealth, Australians and their Environment*, ANU

parties, like lawyers, seeking to demonstrate their perceived value to clients or constituencies, and given their adversarial mindset, can deepen polarisation. A thoughtful and constructive approach can avoid the divorce-lawyer syndrome. One example was the approach of an industry association and their counter party, a major consumer advocacy organisation. In reviewing draft legislation, the leaders of both organisations decided to first document what they had in common in the legislation, and then isolate for attention the limited number of areas where differences remained. It led to a surprising level of agreement, an easier resolution of the outstanding issues and a more constructive modus operandi going forward.

The divorce lawyer problem can be also mitigated by so-called, 'off Broadway dialogue'. This approach seeks to establish dialogue and find common ground away from the media and intermediaries, such as industry associations and activist organisations who feel the need to demonstrate strength to their constituencies.

An important example existed in relations between miners and Indigenous communities. In one case, at a time when conflicts were at a high point over native title between politicians, lawyers, and pressure groups on both sides, industry and Indigenous leaders sat down on country to find common ground. Important issues around land and the environment were discussed at arm's length from the media, with its focus on conflict; and associations executives and 'advisors', who saw their roles as protecting interests.

The polarising public arguments of politicians and lawyers were put aside and the degree of consensus reached surprised both parties. As one senior Indigenous leader said after the meeting:

> Stone throwing through press releases has been unhelpful to all parties involved in the reconciliation process... I think we are on the right track towards building a new way to relate to each other. [The gathering]... was exciting, a very encouraging experience, an important step in highlighting the fact that we share so much in common.[39]

---

39   Dodson, P (1994) quoted in The Allen Consulting Group Report, *Shaping Our Future: Visions and National Strategy Formation*, Economic Planning Advisory Council, Canberra

In Western cultures it is common to assert that individuals or groups have competing sets of values, and that these differences are at the heart of conflict over politics and the role of institutions in our society. Harvard academics George Lodge and Ezra Vogel make an interesting distinction between values and ideologies.[40] They claim that values, such as the need for cohesion, equity and sustainability, are largely shared but that we develop ideologies that tend to separate us. Broad categories might be communitarian or individualistic. These ideologies are formed by our environment, our families, teachers, reading or experiences and provide us with a collection of ideas about how the world works. Lodge and Vogel suggest differences in our influences and experience lead to, for example, conflicting understandings of markets (exploitive or serving human needs) and the effects of government (inefficient and freedom-limiting or beneficial and protective). People consider community issues and policy prescriptions through their own ideological prism leading to a vast diversification of opinions.

The significance of this for corporate affairs practitioners and company managers is to reflect on the origins of our own perceptions of the world and that of our issues adversaries. This means that acknowledging different issue positions can be reached without negative stereotyping and attribution of bad motive. Understanding how each of us with common broad aspirations for our society might come to pursue them differently helps us achieve the constructive empathy necessary for respectful and fruitful debate. Resolution of issues is more elusive if debate starts with the areas of greatest conflict, which is most frequently the norm in policy discourse. Differences are reinforced by the dynamics of advocacy discussed above.

Accordingly, as seen in the cases cited above, it is constructive to first focus and agree on what we hold in common and isolate the (often surprisingly limited) issues that really divide us.

---

40   Lodge, George C., and Vogel, Ezra F., *Ideology and National Competitiveness: An Analysis of Nine Countries*, Harvard Business School, 1987

HIERARCHY OF VALUES

VALUES

- social equity
- social cohesion
- national prosperity
- ecological sustainability

IDEOLOGIES

- values best achieved through individual effort
- competition and markets create prosperity
- government intrudes and distorts

- values best achieved through community effort
- competition can create inequities and markets exploitative
- government includes and protects

POLICY PRIORITIES

- increased competition required to increase economic growth
- faster structural adjustment required
- income differentials required as incentive
- maintenance of a minimal social safety net
- eliminate industry protection
- reduce public expenditure
- internationalise economy
- environment protection through market incentives

- managed, gradual competition required
- staged structural adjustment required
- equal opportunity
- environment protection through regulation
- labour market intervention required
- current social safety net requires extension
- employment

- pace of technological change should be slowed
- broad job creation programs required
- social equity requires active government intervention
- environment preservation requires active government intervention/veto
- industry sectors require protection
- increase corporate taxation and regulation to support extended safety net and control market

CHAPTER EIGHT:
CORPORATE
RESPONSIBILITY

Corporate responsibility is the degree of moral obligation that may be ascribed to corporations beyond simple obedience to the laws of the state.[41]

In recent decades the community has looked beyond corporate economic performance to demand greater business responsiveness to social and environmental issues. International agencies, domestic governments, activist organisations and commentators have sought to raise and codify expectations of corporate responsibility beyond regulatory compliance. As early as 1976, a paper to the Australian Public Relations Institute written by this author stated:

> *There is a widening gap between what business sees as its proper role and what the community expects of it. The community is demanding that business forgo the mere pursuit of profits and are judging companies on their social performance as well as their economic performance... To make a broad generalisation, [business] is not ideologically ready to adjust corporate goals to meet these new community demands.*

The formation in 1974 of the UN Commission on Transnational Corporations, which produced a code of conduct covering a range of corporate behaviour issues, is an early example of global organisations broadening their focus. This was followed in 1976 by the OECD Guidelines for Multinational Enterprises on Responsible Business Conduct of Corporations and Tripartite Declaration of Principles. These principles and guidelines focused on a range of issues including human rights, corruption and exploitation in developing countries.

The concept of sustainability and the environmental impacts of business became the focus of community and corporate attention following the UN Brundtland Commission on Environment and Development which reported in 1987. The report stated:

41   Kilcullen M & Ohles KJ (1999) 'At Least Do No Harm: Sources on the Changing Role of Business Ethics and Corporate Social Responsibility', *Reference Services Review*, Vol. 27 No. 2

It [business] should accept a broad sense of social responsibility and ensure an awareness of environmental considerations at all levels.[42]

There were heightened activities in the early years of this century. In 2000, the UN's Global Compact was launched following UN secretary general Kofi Annan's challenge to companies to join international voluntary initiatives to support universal environmental and social principles in areas such as human rights, labour, environmental protection and corruption. In 2001, the European Commission released a green paper titled 'Promoting a European Framework for Corporate Social Responsibility' which led to extensive consultations, ultimately leading to the development of the European Action Framework for CSR. The commission defined CSR as:

A concept whereby companies integrate social and environmental concerns in their business operations and in their interaction with their stakeholders on a voluntary basis.

As awareness of the environmental and social impacts of companies increased, the language surrounding these issues evolved accordingly. The term 'triple bottom line' emerged to highlight the importance of measuring and reporting on three key areas of business performance: social, environmental and financial.

Following several high-profile corporate governance failures and growing pressure from institutional investors to adhere to comprehensive governance principles, attention shifted to corporate governance. The anacronym ESG was developed to represent the dominant framework for corporate responsibility: environmental, social, and governance performance and accountability.

In 2005, the UN secretary-general asked a group of the world's largest institutional investors to help in the development of 'Principles for Responsible Investment' which encouraged international

42   (1987) *Our Common Future: Report of the World Commission on Environment and Development*, UN

companies to commit to incorporating ESG considerations into their investment practices. It was launched in 2006 and within the decade, more than 5000 companies from eighty counties had signed up.

Around the same time, the intergovernmental agencies, International Finance Corporation and World Bank, initiated the Equator Principles, voluntary guidelines for the financing of projects by major financial institutions. Corporate signatories undertake to advise on and fund only projects that "are developed in a manner that is socially responsible and reflect sound environmental management practices".

The social responsibility movement has not been without controversy. Many political and business leaders continued to advocate the classical shareholder theory. The most prominent proponent of this was Milton Friedman. His view, discussed further in Chapter 5, was that corporate executives should not flirt with CSR, for to do so they must "act in some way that is not in the interests of their employers". He said:

> In a free-enterprise, private property system, a corporate executive is an employee of the owners of the business. He has a direct responsibility to his employers. That responsibility is to conduct the business in accordance with their desires, which generally will be to make as much money as possible while conforming to the basic rules of society. Insofar as his actions in accord with his 'social responsibility' reduce returns to stockholders, he is spending their money. Insofar as his actions raise the price to customers he is spending the customer's money. Insofar as his actions lower the wages of some employees, he is spending their money.[43]

Complimenting this is the view that business makes a sufficient social contribution by creating products people need, providing employment, delivering economic prosperity and paying the taxes that provide government services. Some have alleged companies are

---

43   Friedman M (1962) *Capitalism and Freedom*, University of Chicago Press, Chicago

being pulled off their main game to become 'collaborators' in acts of appeasement to outside pressures such as those mounted by interest groups hostile to capitalism and the market economy.

> *Taking the path of CSR is often presented as a way of disarming opposition to globalisation and capitalism by giving the 'human face'... (some company managers) mistakenly identify the defence of the market economy with making business more popular and more respected through meeting society's expectations.*[44]

Critics of CSR acknowledged that companies must act within the 'rules of society' though they may disagree with some of these rules. Many aspects of corporate responsibility such as corruption, consumer and environmental protection, governance, employment and financial accountability have a regulatory underpinning to some extent. However, the notion of corporate responsibility goes beyond regulatory compliance to voluntary ethical behaviour and the pursuit of community wellbeing.

Governments have maintained a light touch on mandating ESG as an objective of business. India is the only country to impose a statuary obligation, requiring companies spend 2% of net profits on CSR. In Indonesia, company law requires natural resource companies and others "that effect the environment" to implement CSR. In many countries, for example Malaysia and in the EU, mandates are restricted to reporting on ESG activities and performance.

In a prominent legal case surrounding a company's negative social impact in Australia, defence lawyers argued that companies law required directors and company officers to act solely in the interests of shareholders.

The legal case prompted a government inquiry in 2006 to investigate several key issues: the legal responsibilities of directors and corporate disclosure practices; potential obstacles in corporate law that may prevent directors from considering the interests of

---

44   Henderson D (2006) 'Misguided Virtue: False Notions of Corporate Responsibility', *Institute of Economic Affairs*, London

specific stakeholder groups or the broader community in their decision-making processes; and whether directors should be mandated to take such interests into account.[45] The inquiry found that taking into account environmental and social impacts could be accommodated within existing legislation and was not necessarily in conflict with shareholder interest.

At the same time, initiated by the political left, a parliamentary inquiry considered demands for mandatory CSR reporting and regulation to ensure responsible corporate behaviour. The inquiry rejected mandatory action largely on the grounds that 'enlightened self-interest' provided the scope for directors to act responsibly. However, it promoted increased public disclosure of non-financial risks by companies and urged investors, stakeholders, and associations to advocate the inclusion of CSR performance measures as a component of executive remuneration.[46]

Chip Goodyear, the then-CEO of BHP Billiton, the world's largest mining company, commented on the broad conclusions of both these inquiries:

> *The debate around the role of corporations in the community versus their role in maximising shareholder profits seems to fire up again and again. What surprises me is that a debate exists at all. The business case for corporate social responsibility is clear. For BHP Billiton, corporate social responsibility isn't a case of a stockholder versus stakeholder argument but is a critical part of maximising shareholder returns. Simply put, corporate social responsibility is in the best interests of our shareholders and is fundamental to profit creation and sustainability.[47]*

This is a classic statement of 'enlightened self-interest', the idea that corporate responsibility benefits business. This may not satisfy

45 (December 2006) Corporate and Markets Advisory Committee, 'The Responsibility of Corporations'

46 (June 2006) Parliamentary Joint Committee on Corporations and Financial Services, 'Corporate Responsibility: Managing Risk and Creating Value'

47 Goodyear CW (27 July 2006) 'Social Responsibility has a Dollar Value', *The Age*

ethical purists who see business pursuing positive social impact as an end in itself rather than satisfying a business case, or proponents of the 'stakeholder corporation' notion that companies should manage for the interests of a broad range of stakeholders ranked equally with shareholders. (This is discussed further in Chapter 5.)

While governments have generally resisted intervening heavily on CSR, they have welcomed and encouraged developments in corporate transparency. In 1996, as public debate grew, and in response to activist demands, the Australian Stock Exchange published its Corporate Governance Principles and Recommendations. One of its requirements was that companies adopt codes of conduct on ethical and other issues. The exchange did not mandate compliance with the principles but required companies to justify any non-compliance in corporate reports.

Companies had started producing stand-alone environment reports after Brundtland, but in due course these evolved into more comprehensive ESG reports covering a wide range of areas including environmental impacts, the workplace environment, responsibility along the supply chain and practices in international investment.

Initially, companies found it hard to admit to any suboptimal environmental and social impacts in these reports but critics were supportive when companies appeared honest in reporting them. To win and maintain credibility in the eyes of stakeholders, independent validation of reports became common. However, when companies overclaim or are misleading in their performance claims, they are often criticised by the media or interest groups, attacked for dishonesty, 'greenwashing' or, more recently, 'woke washing'. Company regulators are now penalising companies for making misleading environmental claims leading to 'greenhushing', the practice of pulling back on stated green goals for fear of regulatory attention.

While there are several frameworks for reporting, the most widely used internationally is the Global Reporting Initiative (GRI) established in 1999 by a not-for-profit organisation to standardise and quantify ESG costs and benefits of company activities. This has been endorsed by UN agencies and is widely adopted across the Western world. The GRI was developed in parallel with another widely accepted voluntary system, AccountAbility's AA 1000 standards and guidelines, established by the International Organisation for Standardisation (ISO). As with the GRI, these protocols and guidelines are regularly updated to take into account emerging issues and sensitivities.

The growth of various sustainability or reputation indexes, published in the media and influencing reputation and attractiveness to investors, has captured corporate attention. Most noticeable have been the Dow Jones Sustainability Index and FTSE4Good Index that require compliance with a range of ESG criteria. These are discussed further in Chapter 10.

Even if corporate responsibility is not the primary motive behind a company's practices, investors may view it as an indicator of prudent, risk-averse management, especially in sensitive industries. Consequently, alongside pressure from interest groups and their own stakeholders, institutional investors are increasingly compelled to publicly disclose whether and how ESG issues are factored into their investment decisions.

Responsible practice can also be seen as a competitive weapon. The observer of one mining industry company noted its reasons for being proactive on ESG:

> The preference for proactive thinking spilled over into executives' beliefs about early-mover advantage. Noting the high cost of environmental compliance in the face of new regulations [the company] recognised that companies need to be ahead of the group... Since the cost of implementing new government requirements is very high, these companies found it strategic to anticipate government regulation. [The company] expected to enjoy a competitive advantage by avoiding the cost of catching up once regulations came into force. [It] hoped that, by setting a good example through its own operations, it would enjoy an advantage in securing permits for new operations.[48]

48   Dashwood HS (2012) *The Rise of Corporate Social Responsibility: Mining and the Spread of Global Norms*, Cambridge University Press

ETHICAL INVESTMENT

Many individuals are eager to apply their personal values to a wide range of ethical issues, and selecting investments is one way to achieve this. In various forms and degrees of sophistication, ethical or socially responsible investing has been around for hundreds of years. In the seventeenth century, Quakers chose not to invest in the slave trade, and in the 1920s, religious convictions led many to deliberately avoid investments in alcohol and tobacco. In the 1970s, shareholder activism included individuals and investors of university, church and pension funds pursuing corporate social issues through proxy resolutions at annual general meetings. The concept of social investing is now firmly established in the retail and institutional investing landscape.

Inherent to the practice of ethical investment is the willingness to trade off poorer returns for imposed restrictions on investment options. Notwithstanding that, and while it is debatable, some ethical investment advocates have suggested that ethical portfolios have performed at least as well as unrestricted ones, and some claim even better.

Different products are available to ethical investors according to a variety of criteria. Some might prioritise environment, others social issues like tobacco, gambling or alcohol production. Others decide on the basis of labour rights or supply chain issues. And in the USA, birth control and abortion have been prominent.

Funds use different methods to screen companies for investment. Negative screening excludes companies that don't meet specific criteria set by investors or fund managers. Positive screening selects companies whose activities are judged to positively contribute to society, such as those involved in sustainable energy. Some positive screening techniques protect the diversity of their holdings across industries to optimise returns by focusing on 'best-of-sector' companies, those ranked against ethical criteria as the best in each sector.

There are complications and contradictions. A company might score well on workplace relations and opportunities for women but be excluded on environmental grounds. A mining company might be at the forefront of carbon mitigation, a positive for those concerned about the environment, while producing uranium which is a negative for the same investors. A company might score well on gender equity but poorly on other social issues.

As ethical investment funds have become more prevalent, they have attracted increased scrutiny, including from government regulators. Some regulators have even prosecuted funds for misleading and deceptive conduct when they make unsubstantiated claims about their investments.

SELF-REGULATION

While the array of global codes and behavioural checklists for companies emerging from the UN and other institutions have had some resonance, the development of industry and company codes has more practical impact. The adoption of these self-regulatory measures, aimed at protecting industry and company reputations as well as pre-empting government regulation, exemplifies enlightened self-interest at the industry level.

The most influential early industry code was Responsible Care developed in 1987 by the Chemical Industry Association of Canada and adopted by its global affiliates in the International Council of Chemical Associations. It followed an environmental disaster in Bhopal, India, and growing hostility to the industry from neighbours of chemical plants in developed countries. Responsible Care is a series of commitments concerning issues such as safety and the environment and meaningfully consulting with communities. It became a model that was slowly adopted by other industries around the world.

In general, industry associations in Australia were slower than in many developed countries to embrace self-regulatory codes of practice. There are a few notable exemptions, for example, the insurance industry which established a code of conduct as early as 1972.

Most industry associations at the national level require acceptance by companies as a precondition of membership. Some include peer-member imposed fines or other sanctions for breaches of their codes.

Some codes are formally required by regulation or, for example, as a pre-condition for government licencing or acquisitions. See Chapter 12.

Other international confederations of industry associations, like that in the chemical industry, have developed codes but there has also been international activity by companies. For example, early this century an Australian initiative led to the formation of the International Council on Mining and Metals (ICMM). Concerned for the reputation of the industry, a small group of global CEOs met to establish ICMM that mandates a commitment to ten principles covering areas like sustainability and biodiversity, human rights and

Responsible Care Commitment, International Council of Chemical Associations

Through Responsible Care, chemical manufacturers, national chemical industry associations and their partners commit to:

- enable a corporate leadership culture that proactively supports safe chemicals management,

- safeguard people and the environment by continuously improving our environmental health and safety performance, facility security, and the safety of our products,

- strengthen chemical management systems,

- work with business partners to promote safe chemicals within their own operations,

- engage with stakeholders, respond to their concerns and communicate openly on performance and products, and

- contribute to sustainability through development of innovative technologies and other solutions to societal challenges.

Indigenous relations, health and safety and community engagement. Compliance with the principles is monitored independently and regularly. Applications for membership are vetted by independent expert reviews and the fact that there have been considerably more applications rejected than accepted suggests standards have been maintained.

ESG & CORPORATE WOKEISM

While the adoption of ESG commitments by major companies had become a relatively settled issue in the early decades of the twenty-first century, by the second decade it had developed into a politically controversial and polarising topic, particularly after major companies entered debates on general moral and social issues of the day.

Several arguments are offered to support the public engagement of companies in social and moral issues. The first is that politicians and governments are failing to address major global issues and that companies need to step into the void. It is asserted that large companies have resources bigger than some governments and may be better positioned to solve issues like climate change, poverty and human rights. This view was reinforced by findings in the 2023 Edelman Trust Barometer, an annual survey of public opinion in 28 countries.

Another argument for the view that companies should concern themselves with social issues is the concept that businesses have a duty to speak out on these questions. As corporate citizens, it's just the 'right' thing to do.

Observers, for example in the USA and Australia, believe this reflects in part the emergence of a new generation of CEOs that are younger and have grown up in progressive environments, and also, given the war for talent, it is an appeal to a new generation of employees. There is the general perception that young employees or potential employees – the so-called 'Millennials' and particularly 'Gen Zs' – want to 'bring their whole selves' to work and expect their companies to reflect their progressive values.

While some business leaders felt the focus on ESG had gone too

Business Leaders Must Speak Out

Business leaders must not only speak out on incidents of injustice and the pressing issues of the day, but they must take action. There is data from the Edelman Trust Barometer (February 2023) that provides evidence for chief executives to continue to weigh in and lead on societal issues.

- Business is the most trusted institution, by double digit margins over government, in 15 of the 28 countries surveyed.

- Business ranks 53 points higher than government on competence, 30 points ahead on ethical behaviour. Business has risen 20 points on ethics in the past three years.

- On average, 80 percent of respondents want CEOs to speak up and lead on societal action.

- By an average six to one margin, respondents want more business involvement on societal issues such as climate change, economic inequality, healthcare access, and reskilling.

- Nearly two thirds of employees will only work at a company if they share the same values. Sixty three percent of consumers are now belief-driven buyers weighing corporate behaviour in purchase.

- Employees consider their workplace the safest place to discuss societal issues, well ahead of with their neighbours.

far, much of the opposition to it was driven by a political attack on 'woke companies' that were inconvenient to conservative political agendas.

A high point of conflict was reached in 2023 and 2024 when the governments of Florida and Texas passed anti-ESG legislation blocking considerations of ESG factors in investment decisions when government contracts are involved or in consideration of the investment of state funds.

One catalyst for the anti-ESG attack was a highly influential letter that Larry Fink, chairman of BlackRock, the world's largest investment firm, wrote to CEOs in 2019. He asserted that companies should have a social and political purpose beyond making profits. The political reaction was so strong that Fink later de-emphasised ESG in public statements. He said he did so because ESG had "been entirely weaponised by the hard left… and weaponised by the hard right" but that this would not change BlackRock's principled position.[49]

Further controversies broke out as companies increasingly entered public debates on issues such as gay marriage, gender diversity, Indigenous rights and, in the US, reproductive rights. In a heightened political environment, this led to a heated discussion about the appropriateness of companies speaking out on matters that critics asserted were none of their business.

In the buildup to Australia's 2017 referendum on same-sex marriage, the CEOs of 30 of Australia's largest companies, including Telstra, Qantas, Holden, Wesfarmers and the Commonwealth Bank urged the government to take action on gay marriage. Australia's (then) immigration minister Peter Dutton responded, telling the business leaders they should "stick to their knitting" and focus on improving shareholder returns and customer service rather than using their companies to drive personal agendas.[50]

An important issue companies need to address when considering progressive activism is that stakeholders are rarely of one view. There

49   Fink L (14 April 2023) CNBC interview

50   (19 May 2017) Australian Associated Press

is likely to be opposition to positions taken by at least some investors and employees as well as customer boycotts and intervention by hostile politicians.

Some opponents of corporate public advocacy have questioned the competence or appropriateness of companies extending their influence beyond their professional expertise and making value judgements about social and political issues. In doing so, they question whose attitudes and values should be reflected in corporate positions – whether those of mangers or shareholders – although it is rare for companies to take positions without the support of their boards, which were held to represent shareholders.

However, given the level of opposition, there has been increased caution about how, when and on what issues a company should be active in public advocacy. Companies have moved to institutionalise these areas of engagement on issues by establishing processes, protocols, and criteria to ensure that the advocacy does not merely reflect the opinions of individuals but aligns with the company's values and interests. Some explicitly tie advocacy to the company's statements of purpose that, as noted in Chapter 11, are now common and used to drive a consistent approach throughout an organisation. Criteria for decision making commonly includes the relevance of the issue to the business (often interpreted widely) and the expectations of key stakeholders including staff and customers.

Some companies have established committees to consider these issues. In others they are the responsibility of the senior leadership team. In some cases, a broad group of employees is engaged to consider an issue and make recommendations. Employee advocacy groups on issues like climate, gender and Indigenous affairs are common.

Despite facing an aggressive backlash against 'woke' and ESG initiatives, most companies remain steadfast in their belief that they should take a stand on ESG issues and remain ready to engage in areas of public controversy where they deem it appropriate.

CHAPTER NINE:
CORPORATE COMMUNITY INVESTMENT

It is considered best practice for corporate community investment to be determined strategically within an overarching reputation and business-enabling framework in public companies. This marks a shift from the concept of corporate 'philanthropy' to community 'investment' based on business criteria as well as measured social impact. Doing well by doing good. This is being increasingly accepted by governments, shareholders and the not-for-profit sector.

Christian Bennett, Chief Corporate Affairs and
Sustainability Officer, Virgin Australia

Corporate community investment (CCI) is the use of corporate resources for the benefit of the community beyond the production of goods and services. For our purposes, is a distinct concept from corporate responsibility, discussed in Chapter 8, which focuses on responsible behaviour of companies in all their activities.

Historically, companies used the language of 'corporate philanthropy' to describe their contributions to community. This was appropriately distinguished from the use of brand sponsorship of community organisations as a marketing tool. Rationales for philanthropy included fostering employee pride, fulfilling social obligations as responsible citizens, and altruistically 'giving back'. In return, companies expected gratitude, reputation enhancement, the goodwill of the community, and the satisfaction of being charitable.

Generally, public companies designated a pool of funds – or had some ad hoc access to funds – for grants to community supplicants, at the discretion of the company's senior management or the board's donations committee. They were rarely linked to business objectives.

In academic discussion, the view developed that professional managers – as distinct to the owners of capital – had accumulated excessive power and were using the grants to indulge their own personal interests and values in the community and elsewhere. This was particularly common with managerial patronage of favourite causes using shareholder's funds.

Business leaders would sometimes find themselves in a round-robin of obligations across companies, each seeking support for their favourite personal cause and expecting a reciprocal contribution to make. However, directors and CEOs, to divert criticism for indulging in their personal favourites, and to inoculate themselves against unwanted pressures like requests from business peers, found it convenient to hand responsibility for recommending grants to the (then) fledgling corporate affairs function.

High-profile companies attracted thousands of requests, which required them to allocate staff to sift through applications and identify the most worthy. Some companies began to restrict grants to a limited number of specific areas such as education, the arts, public health and poverty relief. The term 'philanthropy' was still used, and the practice was characterised by a 'cheque over the fence' approach with only a marginal relationship between donor and recipient.

This approach still offered loose reputational and other benefits, as mentioned above. However, in the US, the concept of 'strategic philanthropy' emerged, as companies began aligning their charitable contributions more closely with their business objectives. This shift prompted further changes in terminology, moving from 'grant making' or 'philanthropy' to 'corporate community investment' (CCI) or 'social investment,' which suggest a business-oriented purpose and an expectation of tangible returns.

It is important to note the distinction between publicly listed companies and wholly owned private companies where personal interests and disinterested philanthropy may be more appropriately indulged. Similarly, in circumstances such as national tragedies, donations are not considered to fall within the constraints of business strategy.

Studies in Australia and overseas show that many CEOs no longer see CCI as peripheral to business. Apart from meeting community expectations, they are treating it as an integral part of business strategy. Most companies see at least a generalised benefit from CCI, acknowledging that it is often intangible. For many, a more focused business case is assumed or a specific return on investment is anticipated.

REASONS FOR CCI

While most large public companies now require a business rationale for corporate giving, the view that 'it is the right thing to do' continues. It captures the notion of having a stake in society, with obligations and duties as well as privileges, and can be aligned with ethics and behaviour expected more generally of citizens. It also validates the purpose and value statements that companies prepare to demonstrate that they are contributing to social capital and care about the communities in which they operate. These companies recognise that increased interdependence between business and communities is a core part of their business models, necessitating closer relationships that can result from CCI.

Companies are also reporting increasing expectations by communities for various forms of CCI, especially in those directly affected by business location or other impacts. Citizens in the 'anglosphere' – Australia, USA, New Zealand and Great Britain – have been shown to be ahead of other countries in expecting that companies participate beyond their economic contribution to building a better society.[51] Accordingly, CCI can be seen as feeding into a 'community licence to operate', enabling the maintenance of community support for their business activity.

Closely linked to meeting the expectations of stakeholders and maintaining a licence to operate is the issue of reputation. The economic value of reputation is discussed in Chapter 10. The reputation of companies enhanced by alignment with stakeholder needs and interests though CCI can have a positive influence on the way governments, including local governments, deal with them. Not untypically, one company was advised that its bid for an exploration permit was successful, specifically because it had demonstrated strong support for local communities.

Naturally then, companies are seeking to have their CCI initiatives recognised, with a portion of CCI budgets earmarked for promotion. Some are prone to overstate contributions, risking a backlash. On the other hand, some are coy about their community investment. An example of these differences in approach and the consequences involved comes from two major competitors in the resources sector. The CEO of one company, which arguably had the better story, discouraged it being promoted, while the other company made sure

51   (1999) *The Millennium Poll on Corporate Responsibility*, Environomics International Ltd that all stakeholders, including governments, were aware of what they were doing. The latter significantly enhanced its public reputation and politicians constantly praised it in public speeches as a model of corporate citizenship.

Companies will sometimes collaborate on programs in areas of mutual interest. This can occur within one sector when an industry organisation, such as a pharmaceutical group concerned with public health, demonstrates a shared vision. It can be regional, such as support for a local community festival, or a mining company social infrastructure collaboration in a remote area from which staff are drawn.

While it might lessen individual company recognition, joint support for community activities can provide greater depth and quality of contribution, shared administrative burdens and other synergies.

There are numerous examples of companies collaborating on projects with corporate critics or issues adversaries where a common interest can be found. They sometimes seek collaboration with NGOs and activist organisations, motivated also by building familiarity and mutual trust through working together. On some issues, unions can be effective partners, for example when a company is trying to keep local businesses thriving and employing.

This collaborative approach is reinforced by an appreciation that misunderstandings and negative stereotyping is harder when there is some personal connection. Some activists also believe their objectives can be best achieved by working with, and not always against, companies. Examples have included joint management of sensitive forests, the review of product packaging by an environmental advocacy organisation, product design with consumer representatives and field collaborations to map endangered species in conjunction with conservation groups.

In some cases, companies establish research partnerships with government agencies, universities or NGOs to address environmental, public health or social problems. This research is usually aligned with an industry's particular needs or attributes, with a clear win-win outcome in mind. These differ from university collaborations undertaken to solve technical problems for a company.

In recent decades, companies' reputations with their employees or potential employees have been a particularly important driver of CCI. Employees increasingly seek to express their altruism through the workplace and are attracted to companies they see as making a positive contribution to society. This is important for recruitment and retention of socially-aware staff.

CCI activities such as sponsorship of the arts provide opportunities for hosting important stakeholders. Hosting customers or suppliers can be a commercial investment, however hosting socio-political actors, including activist organisations, can also provide a means of establishing contact and building trust.

A less obvious motivation is to expose corporate staff to external perspectives and circumstances as a part of their continued professional development. By working on community projects with not-for-profit partners, and being more exposed to community issues, they become more aware of the environment they are operating in. This should help staff to perform better in their roles. One example is a utility that hosts 'bring your bills' days for customers. Staff meet with customers to explain their bills, provide advice on reducing consumption, and assist with payment plans. The company claims the interaction not only helps customers but gives retail team members a deeper understanding of their communities.

Shareholders of major listed companies seem to support CCI involvements that are reported to them routinely. At a minimum, the return-on-investment benefits of CCI are considered good management, and an increasing number of retail and institutional investors are seeking companies with a high level of social and environmental commitment.

THE NATURE OF CCI

CCI takes many forms at local, national and international levels. Decisions about when, where and with whom to engage are made with strategic intent.

One important criterion for engagement is alignment between the interests and capabilities of the firm or industry and the needs of the recipient. This is illustrated by the pursuit of mutual interests and the deployment of special company skillsets and technologies. For example, mining companies support programs on the environment and Indigenous affairs, particularly where their interests are at stake. They invest heavily in the social infrastructure of communities in mining towns and support services in remote areas such as the Flying Doctor Service. Banks and finance companies support programs in areas like financial literacy and computer literacy for seniors that help to reduce the digital divide and facilitate electronic banking. Insurance companies focus on areas such as neighbourhood security, road safety and renewable energy to protect the climate. Telecommunications companies facilitate help lines, and so on.

Alignment of the special capabilities of businesses with the needs of the not-for-profit sector is most easily demonstrated by the widespread practice of pro-bono work by professional firms such as in law, accounting and strategy development. It can be seen also in the engagement of technology organisations in tertiary education institutions. There they support research, provide equipment and assist in teaching, while gaining knowledge themselves, and interacting with potential graduate recruits.

Opportunities exist for leveraging benefits from existing company infrastructure, intellectual capital or the supplier or customer base. International companies seeking to enter new markets can offer assistance that aligns with the goals of foreign governments. Examples include companies making hygiene and medical products participating in remote areas of developing countries; micro-financing and small business development with company products; and building products companies supplying emergency housing for refugees.

Employees can also become directly involved in community programs. Most large companies have a policy that enables employees to undertake a period of paid leave to volunteer in activities for the benefit of the community. It is not uncommon for these volunteers to bring with them additional forms of support, including modest financial support. Some firms use collective volunteering as a vehicle for team-building and undertake projects like restoring buildings or environmental works. Occasionally, however, accommodating such team-building efforts over the long-term can become burdensome for a recipient organisation, which might then seek offsetting costs.

It is also common for companies to facilitate direct giving to reflect the altruistic aspirations of its staff. In some cases, employees vote for a limited number of charities or projects the company should support financially, and which become the target for their own direct giving or volunteer work. Most companies with these arrangements limit the number of target organisations to simplify payroll management and administration. With staff input they might select categories for employee choice, for example, specifying one organisation in each of the fields of: environment; community welfare; overseas aid; the arts; and public health.

More common is the provision of payroll giving, which allows employees to make regular contributions to their designated cause from their pre-tax income. These contributions are often matched by the company to encourage the practice.

Often, the line between corporate affairs and marketing objectives is blurred. The reputation of a company and the visibility of its community work is relevant to both functions. This is particularly relevant to cause-related marketing and sponsorship, in which a firm promises to contribute financially to causes in proportion to the revenue raised by the sale of their goods or services. This is particularly relevant to retail brands. It can boost employee morale and loyalty while giving exposure to, and benefiting financially, the recipient charity.

Sponsorships can be principally directed to building commercial brands and selling products. Non-marketing sponsorships, however, can be simply used to deliver corporate support to a particular community partner or activity with broader objectives in mind. Frequently there is considerable overlap. Consider, for example, the sponsorship of a major national sporting code aimed at brand visibility but with a wide-spread community program supporting local clubs, enriching local health and promoting community cohesion.

MANAGING CCI

As noted earlier, CCI by major companies has shifted from responses to requests by supplicants, to strategic decision making about the mutual interests of the organisation and the community. Business plans for CCI are established with a clear purpose within an overarching policy framework set by senior management and the board.

Corporate affairs departments, as bridges to the external environment, play a leading role in recommending policy and programs and in managing the delivery of activities. Increasingly, however, community involvement is included in the mandates and performance appraisals of managers, such as those running production sites, and they are obliged to engage in the delivery of programs.

A number of public companies have established corporate foundations to provide focus and visibility to CCI activities, or to centralise giving programs. In some cases, they provide grants independently of the main thrust of strategic corporate CCI. This is the closest remnant of the traditional notion of corporate philanthropy.

Separately identifiable corporate foundations are established with various legal forms with their own benefits and limitations, including their degree of external involvement, taxation implications and levels of external regulation. Regardless of structure, companies will provide support and maintain a significant level of control.

Budgeting for CCI is usually set by the board as part of its annual budgeting process. Some companies contribute according to a formula based on a percentage of pre-tax profits. Decentralised business units or profit centres may have full autonomy over spend levels, while in some companies, decisions are tightly controlled by the centre. Managers in regional areas will normally have modest discretion to contribute to local activities as members of the local community.

One of the most important CCI developments in recent decades is the trend towards having deeper partnerships with fewer external organisations. Companies have concluded that concentrating on a limited number of relationships over longer periods delivers better value for the company and enhances the social impact of the investment.

Criteria for a Successful Partnership Agreement

- Both parties are committed to mutual benefit that can be articulated and understood by each other.

- Neither will be in a dependency relationship to the other as a result of the partnership.

- Both parties can demonstrate the strategic importance of the partnership, beyond the program's immediate objectives and deliverables, to the longer-term achievement of positive social impact.

- Both parties are committed to transparency and accountability in all aspects of the partnership, having the highest regard for individual rights and ethical, social, legal, and environmental imperatives.

- Both parties are committed to a set of principles that include respect, recognition and regard.

- Both parties are committed to a mutually agreeable exit strategy.

- These objectives are articulated in comprehensive and formal contracts which set out mutual expectations and obligations, and criteria for evaluating performance.

Research has shown that corporate budgets for longer-term partnerships weather the storms of economic downturn better than ad hoc short-term engagements. Deeper relationships and ongoing interaction with corporate leaders and staff works best to overcome cultural gaps on both sides and builds trust.

An ongoing challenge is cultural alignment between the business and not-for-profit sectors. Partnerships with community organisations can pose the challenge of bringing together organisations with fundamentally different ideologies, cultures and management styles. Apart from perceived ideological differences, there is often a disconnect between the expectations of quick solutions and hierarchical management structures of business on the one hand, and the consensus-based, voluntarist, and often loosely structured organisations dealing with intractable human problems on the other. Nevertheless, both companies and communities benefit when company resources are deployed by organisations that are closer to the social marketplace and managed by people with a deeper understanding and stronger relationship within that marketplace.

Accordingly, it is important that partnerships are carefully established and based on mutual understanding. This requires the establishment of significant and enduring formal agreements. A starting point is a clear statement of objectives and deliverables with timeframes. Roles, responsibilities and the expectations of both parties need to be clearly defined and articulated, including in the areas of commitments, decision-making processes and protocols around internal and external communications.

Evaluation of social impact is critical to justify the nature, extent and direction of company support. The nature of measurement will vary according to the nature of CCI activity.

The benefits of some types of activity such as cause-related marketing are more easily measured than others. For a company, outcomes might be measured by estimates of tangible return on investment, although they are difficult to precisely calculate. Some rely on stakeholder feedback through surveys, external reputation indices, ranking or benchmarking studies. Whatever method is deployed, companies require some justification for their contribution.

An important but sometimes overlooked issue is the question of exiting an arrangement. Community partner organisations can become dependent on a company's support and the tensions at the cessation of a partnership can negate mutual trust and goodwill if the process is not understood fully at the outset. Best practice for companies is to include protocols around termination of agreements and to commit to assisting recipient organisations to find ongoing alternative support at the end of a partnership.

CHAPTER TEN: CORPORATE REPUTATION

Corporate reputation is perhaps the single most important intangible asset held by a company as it represents the extent to which the organisation is meeting the expectations of its various constituents. The reputation of a company translates into a competitive advantage, is closely linked to its profitability and ultimately affects shareholder value.

The Conference Board

US academic, Charles Fombrun, whose work in the 1990s changed the way businesses think about corporate reputation, defined it as:

> *The overall estimation in which a company is held by its constituents. A corporate reputation represents the net affective or emotional rection – good or bad, weak or strong – of customers, investors, employees, and the general public to the company's name.*[52]

Other definitions anchor corporate reputation solidly to the outcome of behaviour. The reputation of a company informs various stakeholders of what they anticipate will be the company's actions. It is their cumulative expectation. A reputation derives from a company's past behaviour, from its articulation of future behaviour, and whether this can be believed. In other words, reputation is a composite of past behaviour, and the expectations people hold about the company.

Academics will argue over the distinction between corporate reputation, brand and image. In this book, brand refers to products or services – the promise and value proposition the company has with its stakeholders – while reputation refers to the standing of the company as an entity. Both are important to the market and financial performance of an enterprise.

Fombrun suggests various dimensions of reputation relate to both business performance, trust and responsibility. These were incorporated in a system of measurement of reputation as presented to the Centre for Corporate Affairs Institute in 2006.

The various dimensions will be valued differently by different stakeholders. Investors will focus on financial performance and products and services for example, while others will weigh their

---

52 Fombrun C (1996) 'Reputation: Realizing Value from Corporate Image', *Harvard Business School Press*, p. 37

perceptions on citizenship, environmental impact or workplace culture. Some companies will be known for their technical excellence or visionary leadership, or a lack of these attributes. There are conflicting reputations, for example when excellence in financial performance comes at a cost to customer service or the treatment of employees.

DIMENSIONS OF REPUTATION

Social Responsibility
Supports Good Causes
Environmental Responsibility
Community Responsibility

Emotional Appeal
Feel Good About
Admire and Respect
Trust

Vision & Leadership
Market Opportunities
Excellent Leadership
Clear Vision for the Future

REPUTATION

Products & Services
High Quality Innovative
Value for Money
Stands Behind

Record of Profitably
Low Risk Investment
Growth Prospects
Ouperfoms Competitors
Financial Performance

Good Place to Work
Good Employees
Rewards Employees Fairly
Workplace Environment

REPUTATION AS A NON-TANGIBLE ASSET

Company reputation has become a major focus for companies due to the growing appreciation of its value as a non-tangible asset. Good corporate reputations provide a competitive advantage and can have a profound effect on the commercial success or failure of a business. It can impact market and financial performance for various reasons.

First, companies compete to be employers of choice. Recruiters report that potential employees want to understand the values and social contributions of firms when interviewing for a job. A favourable perception of a company reflects on its staff, engendering positive employee morale, so that companies with positive reputations attract, retain and motivate the best talent at all levels. Pride in the company also deepens loyalty and engagement, which leads to higher levels of productivity and discretionary effort. For example, engaged employees are more likely to be ambassadors for a company and deliver a positive customer experience. Conversely, employees can be demotivated when reputations are poor. During periods of reputational pressure, staff in the banking industry have been known to remove company uniforms before travelling on public transport.

Companies with positive reputations benefit from being suppliers of choice and their products and services are sought ahead of others. Some companies seek to leverage their reputations to attract customers by, for example, promoting their social or environmental contributions. Surveys have shown that the public has growing expectations of corporate behaviour and will act against companies that do not live up to expectations. Whether it is consumer boycotts over significant issues or just marginal preferences in a supermarket, customers can reward or punish companies according to their non-product reputation. Suppliers to business customers also benefit if they are trusted and have a reputation, for example, for business ethics, good environmental practices, and workplace management along the supply chain. Both retail and business customers are often prepared to pay a price premium for good reputations.

Companies also seek to be business partners of choice. The reputation of a company is affected by other organisations they associate with as investors or joint venture partners. For example, the reputations of major resource companies have been tarnished by partners in joint ventures acting badly on environmental and Indigenous issues, even when management of the joint venture is not in their control.

Reputation is also essential to building local social licence in communities that companies seek to operate in. Considerable effort is required to ensure a company is welcome in a community, and that operations are seen to create a shared benefit. A positive reputation in a local community can operate in a similar way to savings in a bank account that can be drawn upon in times of trouble. One local community refused to be drawn into media criticism of a company after an oil spill because of the trust and goodwill that had built up over time. However, the converse can also be true. If corporate reputation is low and engagement with the community has been poor, operating and expanding a business can falter. Local stakeholders who provide the social licence to operate can have a powerful voice in government decisions over such things as traffic options, plant siting, and expansion.

A company that has a strong reputation with government will be amongst the first approached when politicians seek views about policy or regulation, or potential collaborations. Access is easier and the company's views get a better hearing. That can make the difference between fighting the rules or helping to shape the rules. Tangible benefits can come from being trusted and from being given the benefit of doubt by politicians and regulators when regulatory intervention is contemplated. In some industries, corporate reputation can mean the difference between detailed scrutiny ('tap-and-tick regulation') and greater autonomy, with effective self-regulation. Reputations are also an important factor in competitive access to land or to licences in restricted industries. Governments don't like to confront local communities and are more supportive of companies that have a reputation for protecting the environment or behaving responsibly.

Considerable work has gone into demonstrating the link between reputation and shareholder value. The fiscal value of reputation, 'reputational capital', makes it easier to raise finance and at a favourable price. Non-tangible assets, such as reputation, are not always explicitly recognised on balance sheets beyond value inherent in brands and goodwill on sale or merger of a company. But studies of equity value have shown that companies with high-ranking reputations have considerably higher stock prices than lower reputation companies.

Increasingly, however, institutional investors such as superannuation funds are applying screens like the Dow Jones Sustainability Indices[53] to measure a company's ESG performance with a mandate to only invest in companies that achieve a certain score or have a tangible pathway to achieving it. One survey used by investors scans the media for negative stories that could impact their decisions. Accordingly, a story that impacts negatively on company reputation can put significant

---

[53] The Dow Jones Sustainability Indices is a family of indices evaluating the sustainability performance of listed companies. It is the longest-running global sustainability benchmark worldwide.

downward pressure on share price.

As discussed further in Chapter 8, a small but growing pool of capital for some companies is ethical investment, which aims to place equity and debt only in companies aligned with the values of investors.

Positive reputations are seen to mitigate various forms of risk, which is important to the price and availability of equity and debt. When recommending stock, investment advisors consider indicators of risk, such as the reputations of the board, CEO and management team, as well as a company's vulnerability to regulators and issues advocates. In a survey for a paper products company, investment analysts and advisors were asked about their attitudes to a company's environmental management. It concluded that environmental stewardship was seen, not necessarily of value in itself, but as a proxy for lowering regulatory risk.

A corporate scandal or accident will usually have significantly negative impact on equity. Share prices tumble rapidly, causing a loss of value well beyond a company's asset values or loss of earnings potential. In many instances, boards and executives are held accountable, and financial and strategic recovery can take many months or years. It some cases they lead to the departure of the CEO and even to corporate collapse. However, companies with strong reputations experience smaller declines than others and are quicker to rebuild.

RANKINGS & REPUTATION MEASUREMENT

It is difficult to measure the economic value of reputation, as it is hard to separate it from other non-tangible assets. It is, however, possible to compare company reputations through rankings. Indeed, this is a popular sport.

Companies are regularly assessed and ranked on reputation by their boards when assessing management performance; by media outlets seeking a story; by consultants; and by other organisations seeking publicity, news content or paid advice to repair them. These public rankings can create a halo-or-horns effect and can influence the way various stakeholders will behave in relation to a company.

As noted above, different stakeholders value attributes of companies through different frames and contexts. The approach of those undertaking a ranking can vary considerably, especially regarding the attributes about which opinions are sought. For a business-to-business company, the focus might be on strategy and management strength, financial and resource strength, technical competence and business ethics. For consumer-facing businesses, attributes such as customer satisfaction, social and community contribution and workplace relationships will be the focus.

Rankings with an emphasis on social or environmental issues often draw heavily on input from advocacy organisations and can be influenced by their biases. Those with a primary interest in financial performance tend to draw on the views of business executives, or exclusively on investors and stock analysts. Accordingly, a fossil fuel company might do badly in one group of rankings but perform well in another. One tobacco company was a 'most admired' company in financial press rankings for several years, while a pariah in rankings by the general public and ethical funds.

Corporate affairs teams closely monitor the rankings of their companies to assist them in stakeholder relations and communications strategies. They also help management teams make decisions. Rankings enable comparisons of companies in general and of competitors in the same industry. The important objective of maintaining reputation is illustrated by the comment of Lauren Fragapane, communications principal at Telstra:

> When it comes to proactive campaign work, we make our decisions based on what will move the dial on our reputation score – it gives us incredible focus.

New technologies are facilitating media sentiment analysis. This is the collection and analysis of information, including in social media, to assesses the emotional tone of comments about a company. It is valuable, given the link between news flow and reputation rankings, and helps measure reputation performance and the finetuning of messages.

Despite the variety of rankings and biases of stakeholder coteries, significant advances have occurred in the standardisation of reputations measurement. After several tracking options competed for the market, RepTrak has emerged as the most common ratings product. Its methodology was developed by, and is based on, the work of Charles Fombrun and Cees van Riel. It provides ratings across seven dimensions of reputation and key attributes of reputation, providing standard measures and actionable insights for boards, management and corporate affairs teams.

While RepTrak is widely used and offers customised information, more forensic examination of a company's reputation can be assessed with quantitative and qualitative research, including targeted stakeholder surveys. Surveys, including reputation audits, can be effective in bringing the perceptions of specific categories of stakeholder to the surface. In one example, using the attributes of reputation articulated by the Fombrun and van Reil framework, the stakeholders (in this case, politicians, regulators, community NGOs and journalists) were asked to rate attributes with values from 1 (poor)

COMPANY REPUTATION WITH INFLUENTIALS

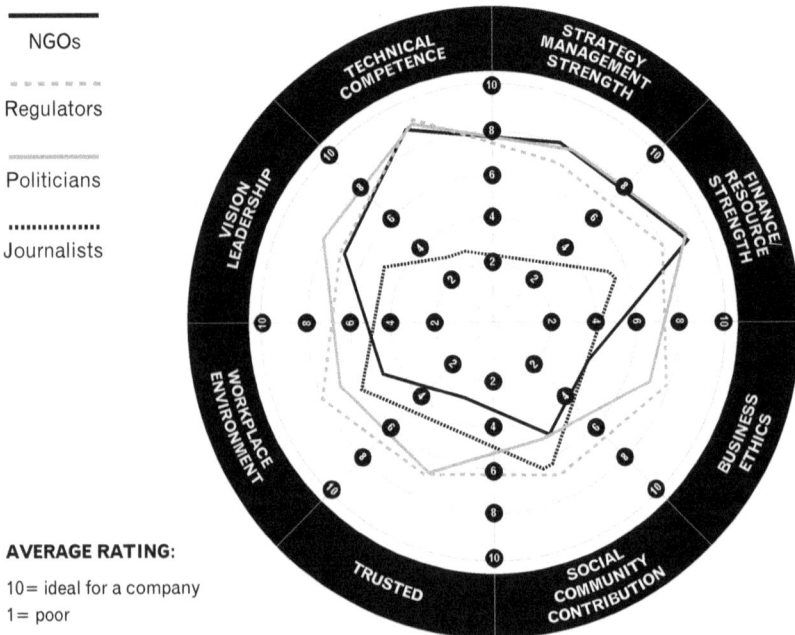

NGOs

Regulators

Politicians

Journalists

AVERAGE RATING:

10= ideal for a company
1= poor

to 10 (ideal for a company). This gave an overall assessment of the standing of the company against those attributes and was easily plotted either in general or for specific stakeholder groups. Respondents were then engaged in discussions to provide qualitative and more granular feedback on the issues of merit and concern.

Respondents can also be asked to rank the company against competitors, to determine their comparative standing within its industry. These comparisons can be represented graphically.

COMPANY REPUTATION – COMPARISONS

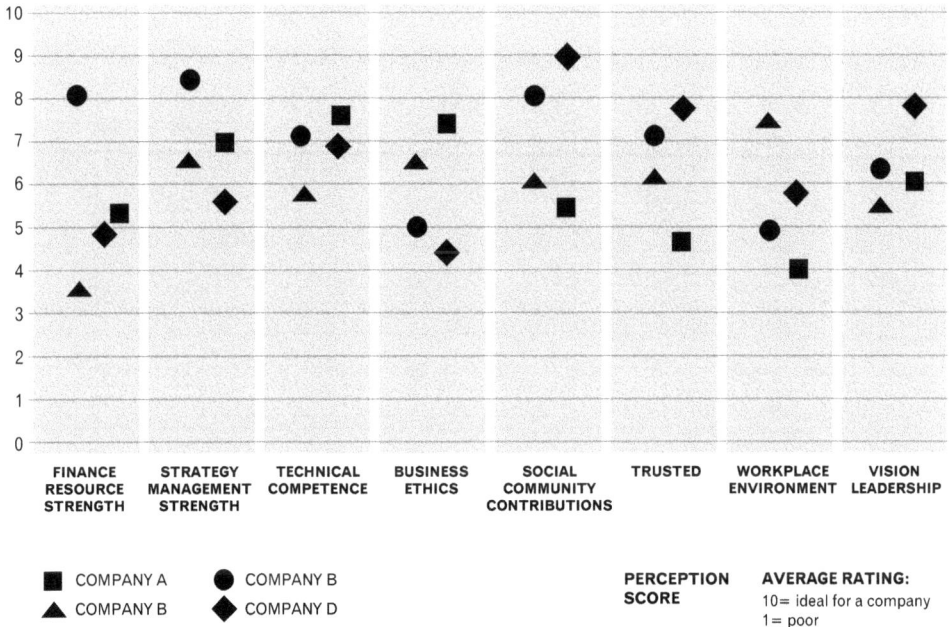

■ COMPANY A	● COMPANY B		PERCEPTION SCORE	AVERAGE RATING:
▲ COMPANY B	◆ COMPANY D			10= ideal for a company
				1 = poor

THE ROLE OF CORPORATE AFFAIRS

Corporate affairs takes the lead in crafting and conveying the corporate narrative. Some companies neglect to tell its positive stories, which can put them at a competitive disadvantage against companies that communicate more effectively. There are numerous examples of companies with exemplary community programs that receive little kudos, while competitors with an inferior story gain acclaim through active promotion.

A firm's reputation depends on its ability to build trust through authenticity and transparency. While corporate affairs professionals might try to shape perceptions, if they do not reflect the realities of the company, a positive reputation will not be sustained. Misleading messages, cover-ups, and greenwashing, for example, are likely to expose a company to new and greater reputational damage.

It is also important that companies understand rapidly shifting societal expectations and the attitudes of their non-market stakeholders. A critical role for corporate affairs is to bring stakeholder views to the attention of management and to help shape business decisions in light of stakeholder expectations. While its external communications function is sometimes called the company's 'window out' to the community, this aspect can also be called the 'window in'.

The role of the function in employee communications, as well as its influence with leadership teams, is essential in ensuring a company's claimed purpose and values are understood and authentically exhibited by all.

The effectiveness of communications is essential to defending a company when it is being criticised or is under attack, and reputational damage from poor communications can make a crisis worse. While reputations can be lost in a flash, they can take months or years to rebuild. When reputations are strong, stakeholders are more forgiving, prone to seeing the crisis as an aberration, rather than endemic.

However, regardless of the starting point, when a company suffers reputation loss, corporate affairs plays an important role in reputation recovery.

A key contribution of corporate affairs in a post-crisis situation is the advice it gives to the board and to the CEO, who is likely to be under intense pressure. Immediate and sustained efforts for reputation recovery are critical. The company needs to demonstrate empathy towards those negatively affected, accept responsibility and provide a clear explanation of what went wrong. It is important to demonstrate what is needed to investigate the underlying cause and to prevent recurrence. This may require difficult decisions to remove elements in the company that can put it at future risk.

Employees are also likely to be bruised and face customer or community pressure. Particular attention needs to be paid to internal communications to support employees and to energise them with company pride and confidence.

Longer-term proactive efforts to rebuild relationships with all stakeholders and demonstrate responsible corporate citizenship assume a higher priority.

CHAPTER ELEVEN: BUSINESS COMMUNICATIONS

The speed and interconnectedness of all aspects of stakeholder engagement and public discourse are being influenced by technology more than ever. From access to digital platforms, expansion of social media, and diffusion of AI, the convergence of these technologies is having a profound impact on both the operating environment for corporate affairs and the skills and capabilities demanded of corporate affairs professionals. This convergence has changed the course of how stakeholders express themselves, to whom, and with incredibly concerning degrees of authenticity and accuracy, and it will require a level of adaption and adoption as fast as these technologies evolve.

John Galligan, General Manager, Corporate External and Legal Affairs, Microsoft Australia/New Zealand

Prior to the emergence of modern corporate affairs, communications (or, as they were then often called, public relations) managers in major companies tended to focus on the limited roles of promotion, publicity and, where necessary, giving the most favourable perspective on a company's position when it was under attack. Their activities were largely writing media statements, speeches and articles for employee newsletters, and answering media enquiries. They were also often seen as the go-to people for events management and other extraneous activities.

The working media referred to them pejoratively as 'spin doctors' or 'corporate flacks'.

While they were often street-smart and skilled at dealing with the journalists many had known as colleagues, these managers were seen as exotic appendages to management and were only fed information as others in the company thought appropriate. They pitched stories for publicity and used their journalistic skills for internal morale building but the role was largely reactive, and practitioners were not in a position to use the media and other communications at their strategic potential.

The 1980s and early 1990s saw a shift in the communications staff from old-style journalists to a new breed of communications executives. Still frequently recruited from the ranks of the media, they tended to be younger, better educated, and more career-oriented. Several had experience in politics and public policy as press secretaries to government ministers.

With this experience, when included in integrated corporate affairs teams, they were more adept at using the media creatively to manage complex socio-political issues and as a tool for agenda-setting activity. Their role became important to both the analysis and execution of issues-management processes at early stages of the issues lifecycle. Their proactive focus helped prepare stakeholders for emerging issues by framing them through the corporate lens.

An important part of the corporate communications task is simply to meet the social and regulatory responsibilities of transparency concerning business performance and activities that affect shareholders and the community.

However, even in routine tasks, significant opportunities exist to help a company define its key communication themes and common threads. This process aids in presenting a coherent, consistent, and easily digestible image of the firm, its values, and its aspirations. This is commonly referred to as shaping, sharing and amplifying the company's narrative. Constructing this narrative needs to be undertaken within the framework of issues and priorities emerging from the company's strategic plan. For consistent messaging, it needs to be crafted and executed in close cooperation with executive leadership including in operating divisions.

To be effective, practitioners working with the media need to demonstrate that they are well informed about the company while being prepared, when necessary, to admit insufficient knowledge and refer media to relevant company expertise. Senior managers are used in media relations in different ways by various companies, taking into account the nature of the issue and their comfort and capability in media environments. The CEO and other company leaders who may appear in the media from time to time need to be aware journalists' agendas and be offered media training.

Turning Things Around

A multinational chemical company was concerned about emerging allegations that an industrial product it had been producing had serious negative health effects on customers. The concerns had become apparent only after a significant lapse of time since the product entered the market. The evidence at the time was by no means categorical and company-sponsored studies were being pursued. The issue had not yet received public attention but was a troubling sleeper for the company. Not surprisingly, it feared serious potential reputation damage and possible lawsuits. It hired top consumer law specialists from a major firm and received conservative legal advice about external relations strategies. The head of corporate affairs was well regarded and well positioned in the company and was able to provide balance to the conservative legal advice in the preparation of strategy should the issue go public. Then it happened.

The corporate affairs executive got wind that the investigative team of a major newspaper was planning to expose the issue in three days with the angle: nasty multinational covers up killer product.

For some time, since the issue had come to its attention, the company had been quietly monitoring former staff and customers who would have been exposed to the chemical to identify any negative effects. As it was an industrial rather than retail product, the company had been able to do a reasonable job at identifying these people, but not all could be found.

Instead of preparing an injunction against publication or denials or other forms of spirited defence, the corporate affairs executive rang the journalists and explained he had heard of their interest. He told the reporters the company welcomed a story and asked them if, through their article, they could help the company to identify those who needed to be monitored.

The issue led the weekend paper as expected, but the angle had been toned down from a story about a poisoning cover-up to an appeal to help find those people who needed to be assessed.

The relationship between the media and communications executives is symbiotic; they need each other. Building and maintaining this relationship requires a similar approach as that used in government relations. It includes creating trust, understanding journalists' needs, and being as helpful as possible. Where it can be achieved, proximity and personal contact is highly beneficial.

In working with traditional media, it is important to understand the different requirements for print, radio and television. Each medium has its own expectations and approach so it is important for media relations executives to understand their individual prejudices and competencies, and develop strategies accordingly.

Proactive strategies to influence policy or public opinion normally require an ability to attract public attention. Some companies have found significant value in taking thought leadership initiatives on issues that concern them. Vehicles commonly used are published research (for example, detailed commissioned research or opinion surveys), speeches reported in the media, and opinion articles or public statements issued to the media via personal and company social media accounts. Chairperson's addresses at annual general meetings are frequently used to deal with issues of corporate concern and to advance public policy or other causes.

One stand-out example of thought leadership was a major address by a mining company leader calling on his own industry to fundamentally change its approach to Indigenous and environmental issues. The speech had significant impact because of its cut-through content, as well as the success of the company's corporate affairs team in broadcasting its message. Another successful example is a major bank's attempt to create a nationwide conversation on national savings policy by publishing commissioned research and getting influential experts to endorse it in a campaign of strategic media interventions. Similarly, a company conducted policy research and used media strategies, along with opinion leader engagement, in a two-year struggle to change an archaic industrial relations framework in its industry. The company educated the public through the media on the impact of industry work practices in order to facilitate acceptance of politically challenging reform.

Companies, however, need to be careful about establishing themselves as leaders on social, environmental or other stakeholder issues by taking a high-profile stance. This can expose them to charges of hypocrisy if or when their own behaviour does not match their rhetoric. Issues advocates are prone to target those corporations making the greatest claims. This has been a problem for companies accused of 'greenwashing' when their actions do not live up to the standards they assert.

Companies have varying appetites for risk when it comes to public exposure and this needs to be considered when corporate affairs teams develop their strategies. Some companies seek to be small targets by adopting a low profile, especially if they feel vulnerable to negative stories. Foreign companies, for instance those in fast-moving consumer businesses, have hidden their corporate identity behind product brands to disguise their foreignness. Taking a low profile limits the opportunity to influence debates on important issues and, in any event, is it not always possible to conceal their identity, particularly in controversial industries.

Another approach that companies, industry associations and issues coalitions use to exert their influence is issues advertising. This is usually done in the print media but also sometimes in television campaigns backed by an active social media campaign. While expensive, this approach certainly generates attention to the issue. The use of advertising for issues advocacy is a specialist field, but several generalisations can be made. For example, televisions ads are not appropriate to present rational arguments on an issue, but can be used to evoke emotions.

A counterproductive use of issues advertising occurred when the enraged executives of one company took out full-page advertisements in major newspapers to rebut, one by one, charges made against it in a TV documentary. Most of the rebuttals were valid and the company's executives felt good about venting their anger. However, the TV program had very modest ratings and the company's response brought the program's allegations to a much broader audience, so that it became the centre of a political controversy.

THE OLD & THE NEW

While these general propositions that apply to traditional media remain, there has been a dramatic shift in the media landscape since the year 2000. The role of traditional media has retreated while new platforms and social media have emerged as the dominant sources of information and opinion-formation. Subsequent loss of market, and consequently advertising revenues, have had a major impact on the economics and available resources of traditional media. This has particularly impacted the print media, with a substantial hollowing out of newsrooms.

With the demands to publish in the competitive 24-hour news cycle, depth and quality of analysis have also been sacrificed for speed. Traditional media conferences and press releases have become less relevant while relentless deadline pressures on reporters and greater reliance on online material, makes it more difficult for corporate affairs practitioners to develop and maintain relationships with journalists. With the possible exception of the finance press, this has been compounded by a decline in specialist journalism (often referred to as a reporter's 'beat' or 'round'). A new breed of less experienced journalists have not been able to develop the commercial understanding required for nuanced business reporting.

Resource pressures on traditional media and new opportunities in social media have led to changes in the activities of media relations practitioners. Online corporate newsrooms have been introduced to provide an authoritative and trustworthy source of company news. They present ready-to-go video, audio, infographics, social media posts, downloadable press kits, clips of key speeches, and podcasts by experts on key issues affecting them. Corporate affairs staff have become their own content producers.

Reduced resources in traditional media can help in some cases for company messages to be published without intermediation. As one senior practitioner put it:

> There are fewer journalists covering rounds in depth. So, the relationship has become less important than being really useful. That means having an excellent understanding of journalists'

needs, their timeframes, and being able to provide as quickly as possible the information and insights they need about your company or industry. Journalists may need to produce a written story for print and online as well as multiple social media posts and even audio and video. What they want and need is content to feed the media beast. Relationships matter but journalists are under so much pressure that it is all about understanding and meeting their immediate needs.[54]

A key role for social media teams is to monitor, through key word search and other digital tools, how the company and its issues are being addressed by others across the various social media platforms. This enables companies to fact check and correct any disinformation bred of ignorance or deliberate distortions by issues activists.

In consumer-oriented companies, the role of corporate affairs and marketing can blur when product and brand issues merge with social and regulatory issues. Companies divide accountabilities and activities in different ways. In some, marketing has the prime carriage of social media with close engagement with social media specialists in corporate affairs. In others corporate affairs leads with marketing accessing its communications channels and working in close association. However, it is now common for channels to be shared and outcomes co-produced to inject corporate messages or positive images into issues running on various social media platforms. Given both internal and external audiences consume information in a variety of ways, messages need to be spread over multiple channels. Both have an interest in maximising engagement even seeking to entertain, as is appropriate to the platform.

There is still an important role for traditional journalism, especially quality print media as a major influential source of news and opinion for leaders in business and government. Respected print journalists and opinion writers continue to have an impact on public discussion.

After several years of turbulent change, major companies have largely adapted to the rise of social media, deepening the convergence of external and internal media as employees actively engage and receive information about the company on social media channels. Given the continuing pace of innovation, responding to rapidly evolving communications tools is an ongoing challenge. This is particularly the case as new applications of artificial intelligence emerge.

AI is making data analysis easier for practitioners seeking to understand differences in stakeholder opinions, find patterns in human behaviour and attitudes, identify issue champions in grassroots networks, and pre-test public policy proposals. It is helping writers, editors and publishers by organising research, producing preliminary drafts of text, and providing illustrations and images for websites, newsletters and marketing materials saving time from mundane tasks to enable greater focus on strategy and creativity. It has been used to predict what aspects of an announcement will spark journalists' interest, as well as their likely attitude and tone.

EMPLOYEE COMMUNICATIONS

In the 1980s, employee communications were largely aimed at instilling a happy working environment. Feel-good objectives, together with information about human resource matters and company activities, were the fodder for in-house publications developed by communications staff.

During the first decade of the millennium there was a short-term shift in emphasis as companies prioritised corporate culture and a number, but only temporarily, rehoused employee communications in human resource departments.

Through the last two decades, the content and purpose of communications with staff has broadened and its carriage shifted back to corporate affairs. As employees receive much of their communication from external sources, it seemed logical that external and internal communications should be managed together with a focus on explaining issues that affect the company. When companies found themselves under siege on environment or consumer issues, for example, attention was given to shoring up internal support or encouraging staff to become 'issues ambassadors'. Staff come under pressure in the community when their companies or industries are under attack and it is important for morale and comfort that they have clear a understanding of the company's position. For a period, this led to the practice of staff being issued with talking points (often referred to as 'BBQ cards') to arm them for peer group discussions in social settings.

However, a shift in emphasis took place in employee communications from top-down information dissemination to deepen staff engagement and interactive dialogue. Internal social media vehicles have helped facilitate this shift. As social media tools and methods were adopted for external communications, they were also called on for use in internal communications. Internal online newsrooms became common and internal social media networks became a valuable tool for two-way and peer-group networking. Webcasts, blogs, and wikis were employed to provide two-way engagement with employees, corporate news and explain strategies. Internal online 'town hall' meeting and facilitated Q&A sessions provide a vehicle to clarify issues and bring to the surface areas of staff interest and concern.

Social media platforms shorten the distance between the higher and lower levels of an organisation. The CEO can post a message and the most junior person can respond without intermediation. They enable online surveys or 'temperature checks' in real time to facilitate rapid leadership responses. However, not everyone is deeply engaged with social media so it is important to use different communication channels with consistent messaging, with language and imagery appropriate to the platform.

An increased focus of internal communications is on establishing and sustaining company-wide cohesion under the rubric of 'purpose'. The concept of purpose was famously articulated by Larry Fink, chairman of investment company BlackRock, in a series of letters to corporate CEOs in 2017 to 2019. The concept goes beyond the business objective of return on investment to improving the world through corporate endeavours.

Experience shows that young people particularly seek to make a broader contribution through their employment and are motivated by objectives that align with their personal values. The benefits of articulating this sense of purpose and embedding it in the DNA of companies include achieving highly motivated employees and supportive customers.

Company statements of purpose are normally couched in aspirational language such as 'to create a better future for customers and the community'. They can be general or skewed to the nature of particular industries. So for a health-related business, purpose might be 'transforming the health of the community' and, for a communications company, 'to create lasting connections that inform and empower'. As one senior practitioner said:

> The way that a business is able to authentically pursue purpose is by understanding it and letting that guide it in terms of both its business strategy and community investments. For example, Origin's purpose is 'Getting energy right for our customers, communities and the planet', and that guides our business… it's actually very real how often we consider decisions against that purpose.[55]

It is common for companies to establish employee advocacy groups to help design its purpose and support its implementation. Examples of advocacy groups include those on diversity, LGBTIQA+, Indigenous issues, climate and community wellbeing. They are typically made up of employee volunteers from any level in the company with varying expertise to canvass and bring ideas together for pursuit by the company. Typically, each is led by a member of the company's senior leadership team, presumably to ensure proposed actions are practical, and to facilitate buy-in from senior management.

While the channels and patterns of employee communications are subject to constant flux as technologies evolve, the fundamental objectives will remain: to align the workforce around shared purpose,

---

55   Samantha Stevens, executive general manager, corporate affairs, Origin Energy

culture and strategy; to demonstrate progress towards shared goals; and to ensure all employees understand how their role can contribute to these ends.

Purpose-Driven Companies

Purpose is not the sole pursuit of profits but the animating force for achieving them... Purpose drives ethical behaviour and creates an essential check on actions that go against the best interests of stakeholders... As (societal) divisions continue to deepen, companies must demonstrate their commitment to the countries, regions and communities where they operate, particularly on issues central to the world's future prosperity. Companies cannot solve every issue of public importance, but there are many – from retirement to infrastructure to preparing workers for the jobs of the future – that cannot be solved without corporate leadership... Companies that fulfill their purpose and responsibilities to stakeholders reap rewards over the long-term. Companies that ignore them stumble and fail... Attracting and retaining the best talent increasingly requires a clear expression of purpose. With unemployment improving across the globe, workers, not just shareholders, can and will have a greater say in defining a company's purpose, priorities, and even the specifics of its business... As wealth shifts and investing preferences change, environmental, social, and governance issues will be increasingly material to corporate valuations.

CHAPTER TWELVE: BOUNDARY FUNCTIONS

While the specific job of public affairs is to monitor and respond to the changing social and political environment, many corporate functions — including legal, human resources, marketing and investor relations — respond to this environment as well. No matter the corporate structure, there needs to be close collaboration wherever functions intersect.

Doug Pinkham, President, Public Affairs Council, Washington, USA

INVESTOR RELATIONS

Until the 1990s there was no dedicated investor relations specialisation in major companies. CEOs and CFOs dealt directly with their leading shareholders, lenders and their advisors. They were advised and supported by former journalists in general communications units that were being progressively integrated into the broader function of corporate affairs. Over the following decade, the largest public companies created specialist investor relations departments – usually within the finance function – to work with the investor community and the financial media.

However, investor relations has become more than just a matter of finance. Important issues can arise between a company and the investment community of direct relevance to the role of corporate affairs.

In the USA in the 1960s and 1970s activists started to target companies through their shareholders. As discussed in Chapter 5 this strategy gained attention when, in 1970, consumer activist Ralph Nader launched his 'Campaign to Make General Motors Responsible'. His team purchased twelve shares in General Motors and issued nine proxy resolutions in a bid to force changes at the company's annual general meeting. Although they represented just twelve of around 288 million shares, the campaign had a significant effect.

Its resolutions called for change to board membership and commitment to a range of environmental, safety and consumer policies. It appealed with some success to several large holders of stock including foundations, universities, pension and mutual funds.

While in voting terms the push was far from successful, the campaign unleashed a widespread public debate on corporate governance and the company was forced to eventually move in the direction of some of the activists' demands.

Targeting companies through shareholder meetings became a common strategy in the late twentieth century as companies were challenged over a range of activities including doing business with South Africa during its apartheid era, weapons production and the environment. The US union organisation AFL-CIO added shareholder activism to its suite of strategies in pursuit of industrial objectives. Its corporate campaign manual stated: "Stockholder actions provide the union with useful possibilities for going on the offensive against the target companies."[56]

Recognising that many labour management relations issues are not appropriate for shareholder consideration, the manual encouraged unions to, "Explore the possibility of submitting resolutions on other subjects, such as the firm's environmental record and/or its finance and investment practices."

This strategy was adopted by Australian labour unions in pursuit of industrial agendas. It also became a key strategy for environmental organisations. The approach was aided by several legislative changes in favour of shareholder rights. As climate change emerged as a prominent issue, resource, energy and finance companies became regular targets.[57]

Most resolutions call for changes in company policy but some, positioned as governance, are directed at enhancing activists' rights to engage with companies on these issues. Organisations involved in shareholder activism make no secret of their intentions. As one with an agenda on climate change declared:

> *We use our shareholder expertise in shareholder strategy to enable institutional investors to escalate their engagement with major heavy-emitting listed companies in their portfolios.*[58]

They can also be shareholder front organisations affiliated with traditional environmental activist groups. For example, Market Forces,

---

56   (2012) AFL-CIO Proxy Voting Guidelines: Exercising Authority, Restoring Accountability

57   Freeburn L & Ramsay I (2021) 'An Analysis of ESG Shareholder Resolutions in Australia,' *UNSW Law Journal*, Vol 42(3)

58   The Australian Centre for Corporate Responsibility

a shareholder activist organisation formed in 2013, is an affiliate of the Friends of the Earth organisation in Australia.

The result of this shareholder activism is that investor relations has become about much more than financial markets, engaging a broad range of stakeholders including small investors and the general public who might be influenced by activist activity.

Some company claims or actions that are intended to please shareholders, such as cost-cutting and high profits, can have the opposite effect on other important stakeholders such as customers, unions or politicians. This arises regularly when announcements of strong profits coincide with high-profile retrenchments. Under pressure from investors on strategy and financial performance, the CEO of a major utility, acting on investor relations advice exclusively, boasted loudly at a press conference about closing country branches in a sensitive election environment, only to receive public castigation by politicians. It was immediately followed by his longstanding commitment to speak at the National Press Club, where the closures became the major focus of journalist attention.

Apart from managing social and political issues, the communications skills and channels used by corporate affairs are called upon to assist the investor relations tasks. The boundary between the corporate affairs and investor relations departments is accordingly sometimes blurred so they require the closest possible collaboration, including joint consideration of strategy, messaging, and seamless execution of communications. Some companies locate their corporate affairs and investor relations teams together to facilitate this collaboration.

LEGAL

Cultural issues and incentive systems can lead to conflict between corporate affairs executives and lawyers, both those employed by the company and external legal experts called in to advise management.

Lawyers naturally focus on the legal arguments surrounding any case and are trained to resolve issues based on the law. Companies are, of course, entitled to pursue and protect their legal rights. However, a company's interests are not always best served by their pursuit.

There are situations when pursuing a company's rights in law can be counterproductive and legal action can lead to 'home goals'.

Corporate affairs is more concerned with the long-term impact on companies of perceptions than legal entitlement and seeks to resolve issues with the least damage to reputation and stakeholder relationships. The two approaches to the management of issues have the potential to clash and can lead to conflicting advice.

Litigated outcomes that support a company's position, especially when a powerful corporation has a win over a smaller or perceived-to-be weaker adversary, can lead to public disfavour. A high-profile example emerged when two London activists refused to apologise for distributing pamphlets critical of the fast-food chain, McDonald's. The company sued the pair for libel. The activists had few resources but attracted considerable pro-bono support and the case became

Legal Self-Harm

For two years, a major Australian bank featured in frequent tabloid headlinesfor using legal manoeuvres to avoid the publication and tabling in parliament of damaging internal correspondence, fearing it could lead to successful litigation by customers. As the media and public looked on, the bank frantically tried to plug ever-developing holes in its non-disclosure dyke. It appealed to the law. In one newspaper advertisement, the bank stated:

> The legal position which the Bank has taken in relation to these letters has been endorsed by the courts... [We are] not willing to endanger the effective operation of the judicial system.

It was a reputational disaster. Commenting on the ultimate reputational and business damage caused by the attempted cover-up, the CEO later admitted the bank's strategy was flawed in part because "the lawyers wouldn't let me speak".

an international cause-celebre. With over 313 days of evidence and submissions, it became the longest running case in UK legal history. The courts deemed some of McDonald's claims to be true but with the defendants calling 180 witnesses to dump on the company, the ongoing and relentless publicity painted the picture of McDonald's as a bullying giant. The legal arguments were obscured by negative stories and sympathy for the underdog.

In an Australian case, a forestry company sued twenty defendants, including a high-profile politician, over alleged harassment concerning a pulp mill. However, the assertive action by the company attracted national and international attention, motivated a large number of additional protestors, and brought into play other interest groups worried about any legal precedent that would limit their activist tactics. Settlement eventually took place out of court with costs awarded against the protestors, but nobody felt the legal action benefited the company.

In numerous cases, reputational and other costs to a company have far outweighed the benefits of legal strategies. In so many areas of corporate affairs, the way an issue is managed can be more important than the issue itself.

Activists have discovered the effectiveness of strategic litigation in their campaigns and adopted various types of 'lawfare' such as test cases, class actions and third-party appeals, winning legal standing in pursuit of their causes.

These legal manoeuvres and the strategic use of the media to comment on proceedings, disliked by the courts and eschewed by conservative lawyers, are less available to major companies who the public hold more accountable than activist groups for their actions and statements. These factors plus the David and Goliath sentiment in public opinion requires more than a reliance on black-letter law.

A major mining company suffered serious damage because of an environmental issue and subsequent class action in a high-profile joint venture in Papua New Guinea. Some local communities were concerned about environmental damage and called in plaintiff lawyers who launched 'litigation patrols' to sign up local villagers to a class action with agreements that gave them total control and a large success fee. The lawyers engaged churches, unions, and environmental groups to support their case, shaming the company aggressively in the media. With little initial involvement of the company's corporate affairs team, the plaintiff lawyers effectively framed the issues in public perception through the media. In contrast, the company and its conservative legal advisors relied on the law while interpreting these extra-legal pressure activities as sub-judice. They eventually settled out of court but the legal outcome was overshadowed by years of reputational damage and eventual disinvestment of the asset.

Over recent decades, however, in-house company lawyers have become more conscious of corporate affairs perspectives and while differences in mind-set persist, holistic approaches to the management of legal issues have become more common.

The question of legal liability is often linked to a company's insurance coverage, an added obligation that limits the freedom of companies to respond to problems. The corporate affairs instinct is to show regret and concern through statements and actions regardless of fault. This is often discouraged as it can be seen as detrimental to any subsequent legal challenge. A solution in the case an oil spill the company believed was caused by another party, was for the CEO to declare:

> My lawyers tell me we were not to blame but we are very upset by the incident and will act to rectify the situation as quickly as we are able.

REGULATORY AFFAIRS

Corporate affairs departments interact frequently with legal departments on regulatory affairs and compliance. In some industries the regulation is technical, involving economists and technical specialists, in which case legislative affairs are sometimes driven by stand-alone regulatory affairs departments with legal and corporate affairs departments playing supportive roles.

However regulatory issues are managed, relations with regulators have legal, technical and corporate affairs dimensions and, again, professional cultures can clash.

For corporate affairs, the government relations toolbox is employed in building and maintaining relations with regulatory agencies. Most regulators will seek to achieve the corporate behaviours they are required to uphold through collaborative means, even to the extent that some critics allege they are captives of the industries they regulate. With appropriate relationships, regulators are able to provide guidance on the application of the law and explore solutions to their concerns that avoid penalty or litigation. While retaining their rights and entitlements in law, companies with a corporate affairs mindset will try to resolve issues through cooperation and the search for positive-sum solutions with regulatory authorities.

Telco Versus the Regulator

In the context of major changes in the industry, a major telecommunications company came under the leadership of several US executives who had an uncompromising and combative approach to dealing with government and regulators. In public statements they pilloried the government and called the competition agency 'rogue regulators' and 'maggots'. Rather than co-operating with regulatory authorities, they fought them at every opportunity with an array of costly legal challenges. The company's pressure tactics won them some points in law, but politicians were keen to punish them for their confrontational approach, and regulators gave little ground. Paul Fletcher (who later become Australia's communications minister) noted in a book on the saga (*Wired Brown Land*, 2009) that the company was subsequently dealt 'a thousand cuts'. He used the case to illustrate counter-productive consequences of its confrontational strategy. On their departure, the board appointed a CEO with a totally different approach who established a more trusted and sensitive relationship with its regulators.

Lawyers have responsibility for ensuring corporate behaviour complies with the law and regulations as well as protecting a company's rights and entitlements when they are challenged by regulatory authorities.

The propensity of some lawyers is to play hardball with regulators by, for example, aggressive assertion of legal argument. In many cases this is appropriate to protect a company's rights, however there have been examples of confrontational corporate tactics that are counter-productive, leading to regulator distrust, enhanced scrutiny and subsequent retribution.

A major area for corporate affairs involvement is industry and corporate self-regulation and codes of conduct. The function plays a role in helping develop these codes, ensuring understanding and compliance with them, and liaising with government agencies on their operation.

Codes of conduct can be initiated from business to stave off government-imposed solutions to issues, or from governments (through legislature or regulatory agencies) as a precondition for licences or to facilitate flexibility in achieving regulatory objectives.

They are sometimes completely voluntary, but government has a role in quasi-regulation and co-regulation. Quasi-regulation describes those arrangements where government influences business to comply, but do not form part of explicit regulation. This normally covers areas where governments are likely to intervene and mandate behaviour if "a self-regulatory scheme does not exist or may regulate in the future if the self-regulation does not demonstrate its responsiveness to community expectations".[60] Co-regulation typically refers to situations where industry develops and administers its own arrangements, but government provides legislative backing to enable the arrangements to be enforced.[61]

---

60   Australian Law Reform Commission (2023) 'Classification Content Regulation and Convergent Media' *ALRC Report 118*

61   Australian Law Reform Commission (2023) 'Classification Content Regulation and Convergent Media' *ALRC Report 118*

CORPORATE AFFAIRS & MARKETING

There are often differences between the mindsets and incentive systems of marketing and corporate affairs departments. However, many of the skillsets and techniques are held in common.

Marketing is undertaken by a company to promote and sell its products or services. A company's reputation, behaviour and its perceived environmental or social impacts (areas of primary corporate affairs concern) can have a significant effect on its ability to sell its goods and services. However, the approach marketing takes can also influence perceptions of a company and can impact its standing with stakeholders other than customers, including neighbours, politicians and regulators.

In addition, many areas of activity overlap. Corporate community investment, the province of corporate affairs and cause-related marketing (CRM) is the most obvious. Both are aimed at assisting the community and building reputation while CRM is aimed more directly at expanding sales. Examples of CRM are donations to local schools or charities in return for shopping volumes in local supermarkets. More subtle examples are aligning product promotion with social movements such as a rejection of beauty stereotypes, or associating products with positive environmental features.

Both corporate affairs and marketing take a considerably different approach in fast-moving consumer goods companies whose focus is on retail customers, than those whose customers are largely other businesses. In the former, marketing tends to get much bigger budgets, including to support advertising, and clever corporate affairs departments find ways to leverage some of that to further their stakeholder relations objectives. In these companies, corporate affairs supports marketing while managing corporate reputation and issue management aspects of marketing activities.

Corporate sponsorship in sports or the arts can be either motivated by marketing or be part of a corporate affairs community investment strategy. They (marketing and corporate affairs strategies) are interdependent. Sponsorship of a major sporting code or performing arts company for brand awareness will create opportunities for hospitality with public policy influencers and others and spill over into funding of grass-roots community development programs.

Marketing activity that is insensitive to the social and political environment can have negative impacts on the task of corporate affairs managers. As one senior corporate affairs executive said, "At its best, corporate affairs scans (marketing) proposals to help avoid and manage reputation damage. At its worst, corporate affairs manages the fallout." [62]

Marketing departments can be wary of corporate affairs, for example in its social media activity, and corporate affairs practitioners can resent scrutiny by what they call 'brand police'.

A classic case was the proposal for a high-profile campaign to market fruit-flavoured alcoholic mixers to the young adult market at a time when heavy restrictions on alcohol marketing was being considered by government. The company's corporate affairs became aware of the campaign late in its development and raised concerns. The CEO intervened and the campaign was abandoned.

There are many concepts and processes in the marketing toolbox of direct relevance for the corporate affairs practitioner. These include targeting and target segmentation, analysis of stakeholder expectations, and behaviour and message development through market research methods including the sophisticated use of data analytics.

There is no closer area of interface between marketing and corporate affairs than in social media. Whichever function leads on social media, channels are shared and messages are often simultaneously infused with both marketing and corporate affairs content.

HUMAN RESOURCES

The employee communications role has moved between corporate affairs and human resources (HR) departments. There are points of overlap and internal channels are frequently shared.

---

62   Rob Hadler, former head of corporate public affairs, National Australia Bank, Coles Group Ltd and other companies.

Corporate affairs interests and modus operandi in relation to employee communications are discussed in Chapter 11. In summary, internal communications are designed to build an understanding of, and commitment to, a company's purpose, values and objectives, and to engage employees on issues of their concern.

Corporate affairs departments, in cooperation with HR, have a strong interest in the content of training employees. It is important that a company's culture overall is sensitive to its social and political environment, and staff are aware of the issues that can arise between the company and its stakeholders. It is also important that executives and all staff, through training and professional development, understand the role of corporate affairs and its relevance to their day-to-day activities.

Given its significance, it is surprising that the broad sweep of issues related to corporate affairs management are often omitted from induction, trainee and general management training programs run by HR. It is important not only that corporate affairs leaders ensure due weight is given to these matters in general but that they provide appropriate support and resource materials to assist training and development.

Job rotation can be an important element in staff training. Rotating staff from general management and other functions through corporate affairs departments is a useful way to spread skills and awareness. Some enlightened companies have required their 'high-potential' executives to work for a period in corporate affairs, given the significance of external relations issues for senior management and especially CEOs. A growing number of CEOs of major companies started their careers or spent considerable time in corporate affairs departments.

Conversely, as discussed elsewhere, it is important that corporate affairs staff have a broad understanding of business including its language and drivers. Overall management training including production, marketing and finance should be part of the development of the corporate affairs professional. This can be deepened by temporary location of corporate affairs staff, where appropriate, in other departments of the business.

CHAPTER THIRTEEN: PRACTICE MANAGEMENT

Strategic public affairs... goes beyond knowing the business to being a true business partner, taking action to anticipate problems, to smooth the way, protect operations and mitigate risks. As a leadership function, its role is also to create opportunities including to proactively impact both the business model and/or the socio-political environment in which it operates.[63]

LINE MANAGEMENT RELATIONS

The relationship between corporate affairs and line management is critically important.

The role of the function's professionals has grown over time, at best practice culminating in their engagement well before significant corporate decisions are made. It is now normal for the heads of the function to be members of senior executive committees at the corporate level or regularly involved in their discussions. Almost always, corporate affairs is represented on business unit executive committees, and its leader is a member of the company's senior leadership team.

However, the function's emergence has by no means been uniform across companies and locations. Its full development has been more common in larger companies and those with the greatest threat from social, political and regulatory challenges.

As a generalisation, there are three basic approaches to the role and positioning of corporate affairs in firms ranging from the basic to the most influential and strategic. They represent the evolution of the function since the 1980s towards achieving its potential in high performing companies. At each level, critically important contributions to favourable business outcomes can be made.

The first and most basic level of corporate affairs can be called the 'transactional' level. Here the function is sometimes seen as a 'problem dump'. The role is often reactive, helping the company put out fires as they emerge. A cartoon describing the function depicts a practitioner in a glass box with the inscription: 'PR – When in trouble, break glass'.

At this level the function can still be proactive in pursuit of the company's image and reputation. For example, promoting the company in the media, crafting messages for various stakeholders, organising events and assisting in speechwriting.

When practitioners principally operate as just defenders and image makers they are seen as somewhat exotic to others in management and not accepted as general business executives. They are considered to have specialist skills without a deep understanding of a company's technologies, finance or markets.

At this first basic level, corporate affairs practitioners are likely given information about company thinking on a needs-to-know basis and will only be briefed with information more senior executives consider is relevant to them. Accordingly, they tend to acquire only incidental knowledge of the early stages of corporate planning or once decisions are made and directions are set. As a natural consequence, their skills and connections tend to be deployed at a late stage in the issue's life cycle, reacting to agenda and issues framed by others. This prevents the company from capitalising on strategic opportunities that might have been available earlier. Any corporate affairs planning is likely to be pursued on a narrow functional base, focused on activities or inputs, rather than strategically driven by major corporate priorities.

During normal business periods, the importance of corporate affairs may not be apparent and the function may seem expendable. External providers could be seen to reasonably provide ad hoc support both for crises and more mundane matters. Activities such as building non-market relationships, developing data for use in advocacy, educating the public and governments, and working with line managers to learn their issues, are often seen as non-essential by operations managers who do not understand the contribution the function can make and have not had a crisis to jolt them into reality. It is also common that areas now accepted as sub-functions of corporate affairs are not integrated but separated into silos or allocated to other units such as internal communications with HR or government affairs with legal or regulatory affairs.

The second level of corporate affairs can be called the 'consultant' level. As well as the activities described above (an integral component of the function), the corporate affairs manager is called upon to provide more strategic advice as a resource or consultant to line management. In some companies this 'client-provider' model, which frames corporate affairs as a business service function, has resulted in it being relegated to a 'service centre' role, again only called upon when it is seen by other managers to be needed.

It is not uncommon for regular consultations to take place between corporate affairs practitioners and line mangers to determine the nature and extent of services required by the manager, which becomes a major influence on the function's budgeting and resource allocation. Sometimes this has also led to full cost charging to business units and, occasionally, even contested bidding for services with external providers.

Under the concept of consultant to line management, practitioners are provided with information that is seen as relevant by their business 'clients', who are less equipped to understand what is relevant in the social and political environment. This limits the potential of corporate affairs to provide input to strategic business planning. As in the first level described above, when the function operates just at the consultant level, the company is not well positioned to identify issues early, to take the initiative in framing them, or to have the best opportunity to shape outcomes.

The third level can be called the 'strategic' level. While the basic communications and advisory functions discussed above still need to be performed, at this level senior corporate affairs practitioners are fully integrated into the senior councils of the company and are accepted as fully-fledged business executives. As senior members of the leadership team, they contribute to decision making and forward planning.

Corporate affairs teams at this level holistically combine sub-functions of communications, public policy and government relations, stakeholder relations and community investment, as well as (non-technical) sustainability activities.

At this strategic level the contribution of corporate affairs is valued because there is a reasonable understanding in senior management of the significant opportunities or vulnerabilities resulting from the way social and political issues are managed. There is respect for the practitioner's knowledge of how the company's stakeholders will be impacted and how they will react to corporate actions. And it is accepted that identifying issues and managing relations with governments, key opinion leaders, issues advocates, and local communities can create competitive advantage over issue opponents or business competitors. By noting trends in the non-market environment and in stakeholder attitudes, and by creative use of public policy and regulatory relations, corporate affairs can not only help prevent or resolve problems but also generate new business opportunities. As the CEO of one major company said:

> In essence they [corporate affairs executives] are the acknowledged authority on the social and political environments and their effects on our business. As such, they are playing an increasing role in planning, issues management and the creative use of public policy to further company goals.[64]

Accordingly, while a range of basic activities or sub-functions is required, the role of corporate affairs is to help to find optimum alignment between company plans and their implementation, and the imperatives of the social and political environment. Its work should be fully aligned with corporate strategy and focus on short, medium and long-range horizons for issues and opportunities.

EVOLUTION OF PUBLIC AFFAIRS

	TRANSACTIONAL	CONSULTING	STRATEGIC
ROLE	PR and troubleshooter	Management resource, consultant	Strategic business partner
INFORMATION	Need to know	Need to know	Seat at strategy/ planning table
ORIENTATION	Largely reactive	Reactive proactive	Proactive opportunistic
TASKS	Task driven	Expert advice	Strategic analysis creative solutions

Studies have shown that CEOs tend to have a greater understanding of the nature and value of corporate affairs than line and other staff managers. This is understandable considering that so much of a CEO's activities involve external relationships including engagement with non-market stakeholders. As one business leader stated, the CEO "has to worry about all the things that happen outside the company".

However, as social and political issues have increasingly impacted business outcomes, pressure has mounted on line managers to accept ultimate responsibility for stakeholder relations, reputation and the day-to-day management of non-market issues impacting business activities. Business statesman Sir Arvi Parbo made the point:

> *It is important that we value the capacity to deal with the social and political environment as an important part of the abilities which go into making a manager. Performance in this area must have increasing weight in the way our managers are recruited, trained, evaluated and rewarded, because of the critical nature of these issues to the success of our enterprises individually, and indeed of the whole free enterprise system.*[65]

Consequently, management of external relationships, along with financial and other criteria, is being introduced into managers' job descriptions, performance appraisal and remuneration at-risk. This broadening role enhances line managers' understanding of the need to harness the resources of corporate affairs, and strengthens the role of corporate affairs as coach and advisor.

BUSINESS & CORPORATE AFFAIRS PLANNING

At best practice, corporate affairs is connected at all levels to corporate and project-planning processes. The function can contribute to an understanding of the future non-market environment and potential risks and opportunities, and can recommend risk mitigation and other relevant strategies. As discussed above, this requires access to timely

---

[65] Sir Arvi Parbo, chairman of Western Mining Corporation, launching the Centre for Corporate Public Affairs 1990.

information about plan intentions beyond what other managers in the company may identify as relevant for corporate affairs. In large companies with strategic planning departments, corporate affairs executives should establish the closest possible relationships with them.

In some companies the function prepares an assessment of the social and political outlook for a project or planning period, which is included in the documentation to provide context and highlight issues needing attention. This analysis sits alongside the economic, market and competitor analysis. A similar contribution can be made by submitting business plans to social and political stress testing and by assessing them, for example, against forward-looking stakeholder and issues audits.

While adding value to a company's strategic plan, most important driving imperatives rising from that plan should be the starting point for corporate affairs' own function planning. This contrasts to 'bottom-up' planning that has traditionally taken place in sub-function silos. With government relations, for example, the bottom-up process might be for the plan to establish relations with X actors, or to prepare Y briefs or Z position papers. For community relations it might be to establish advisory committees or conduct stakeholder audits. These will be all relevant and important instruments to deliver a company's strategic objectives but, at best practice, corporate affairs plans are developed in an integrated manner around priority business objectives, priorities and strategies. Accordingly, whether a company's strategic priorities are to pursue an acquisition, enter a new market, undertake corporate restructuring, or open a mine in a local community, sub-function plans should be written in conjunction with each other.

For most, this will require government relations, media relations, community relations, internal communications and probably community investment as integrated tools for the facilitation of these business objectives. The focus on strategic outcomes rather than products or processes ensures discipline is maintained in pursuit of priorities and optimises the use of resources.

The function's plans should specify timeframes in which objectives are to be achieved and, where possible, criteria and metrics by which performance can be measured.

Notwithstanding the strategic intentions of function plans, it would be naive to assume that priorities won't change or that the environment will not throw up unpredicted situations and challenging issues that will need attention and call on resources. Some can be foreseen by effective issues management, but planning will require flexibility to accommodate them. It would also be naive to think that line managers will not confront issues and seek support that is beyond what has been anticipated. Signed-off plans with clear priorities better equip corporate affairs managers, however, to push back on low-priority demands for corporate affairs time and resources.

STRUCTURE

Given the importance of CEO engagement with non-market stakeholders, and the significant extent to which a CEO is engaged with them, close relationships between the CEO and senior corporate affairs executive should be the norm. In many companies the head of corporate affairs is a direct report to the CEO. However, as companies expand and CEOs seek to limit their direct reports, the head of corporate affairs may sit in the next line in the hierarchy. Where there is not a direct report to the CEO, corporate affairs leaders have full and frequent access to the CEO and relationships can become close. As Wesfarmers CEO Richard Goyder told a business audience, "I have my two harshest critics here tonight, my wife and my head of corporate public affairs." And as one newspaper editor said, "You can tell how well the company will manage these things by the proximity of the corporate affairs leader's office to the CEO's."

Normally, access is also readily available to the chairman and board. It can be seriously counterproductive and detrimental when, as sometimes happens, corporate affairs advice is presented in executive committees through intermediaries who have a sub-optimal understanding of the function.

Corporate affairs departments are structured differently across companies and in different parts of the world. In the USA and parts of Europe, communications has been managed separately from government relations, and corporate responsibility or community investment is separate again. This reflects different business cultures and government systems.

The integrated function, sometimes referred to as 'the Australian model', is emerging globally as best practice. Successful management of significant issues normally requires a holistic approach to the external social environment and political system. Corporate and industry reputation in the community generally impacts business legitimacy with both commercial and political consequences. Traditional and social media is both influenced by, and has an influence on, the articulation and development of issues with all stakeholders including staff, investors and government. Local communities can exert political influence and can veto, delay, or lead to costly conditions on development. Employees need to understand issues facing an organisation and the company's approach to those issues, especially where they are controversial. Accordingly, the integrated function appropriately combines government relations and public policy with other sub-functions – the various forms of communications, issues management, reputation management, community investment and stakeholder relations. As discussed in Chapter 12, corporate affairs departments sometimes include investor relations and regulatory affairs, but where these are managed externally to the function, they work closely and their work is co-produced.

A company's structure and its approach to reporting lines and profit centres will all vary according to the industry or the organisational philosophy of the latest CEO or organisation consultant. Companies in industries with higher vulnerability to socio-political pressure are more likely to have large corporate affairs staff, resources and sub-function specialists. Demands will be greater for market leaders than other companies in most industries. Some, such as major info-tech companies, initially underestimated the relevance of corporate affairs. However, they were forced to quickly build large corporate affairs teams when they faced non-market headwinds.

Major issues arise around centralisation, decentralisation and the complexities of matrix organisations, particularly with international operations. Some companies have no need for corporate affairs staff outposted in business units and can run the function wholly from the corporate centre. Those who are not 'issues rich' may be able to operate with one broadly skilled, multi-tasked executive or small team in the corporate office. Few companies can afford to replicate all the sub-functions in their various business units. In decentralised businesses it is common to locate a functional generalist remotely in projects or business units to work in coordination with sub-function specialists at the corporate centre as needs arise.

Tensions between business units and corporate headquarters are not uncommon, and these arise within the function as well as more generally across a company. Some business units complain they are not getting the support they need from the corporate centre. They can be tempted to involve external consultants who risk bringing different, even competitive, agendas and who are not linked, or committed, to a cohesive corporate approach. Critically, they carry no responsibility if a crisis response is not effective or errors are made.

Dual reporting lines, where employees report both to the business unit leader and the corporate affairs leader, or across international business units, are common. However, these can create challenges when the priorities and approaches of their superiors conflict. Corporate affairs executives in business units can get caught up in company politics including rivalries over strategic directions, competition for resources or CEO succession.

Decisions need to be made about where responsibility for managing any issue lies, for example, in a business unit or at the corporate level. Issues-management systems should be company-wide but, within that, business units will have their own specific responsibilities and issues slate. Issues that arise in business units may be contained there, but overall corporate reputations can be impacted by even the narrowest unit of a business (in one example, a few rogue currency traders in a major bank cost the jobs of the

CEO and chairman). Business unit issues can escalate to impact the whole company because of a failure to effectively manage them locally, or because of the tactics of issues adversaries. Decisions are then required to determine when to escalate the management of the issue to the corporate level.

There are many instances of failed coordination, especially in highly decentralised businesses. For example, two divisions of the same company once approached a government minister with contradictory proposals, unaware of each other's actions. In another company, after the CEO instructed business unit leaders to strengthen relations with the state government, the premier's chief-of-staff called the CEO's office to ask which of the company's dinner invitations the premier should accept for the same night.

There are obvious means to maximise cohesion and coordination including coordinating committees and systems for knowledge management and regular information sharing. Flexible movement of staff and the formation of issues teams across disciplines can help cohesion. When specialisation in a sub-function emerges in a business unit rather than in the corporate centre, that expertise can be deployed elsewhere in the company. In one example, a corporate affairs practitioner in one business unit developed expertise and experience in crisis management after several incidents, so was later able to lead crisis management in other parts of the organisation.

Most important is a strong climate of goodwill within a company-wide corporate affairs community of practice.

Reporting lines and performance appraisal of corporate affairs employees across the company can be important in maintaining discipline and cohesion. Corporate alignment can be influenced by the corporate head of the function being involved in both the appointment and remuneration at risk of outposted corporate affairs staff.

Problems in cohesion can be exacerbated by the appointment and management of external providers, particularly at a distance in business units. While it can be a useful source of expertise or objectivity, for example in stakeholder audits, outsourcing is in practice more often driven by overflow work, cost-saving and resource management than strategic input. External economic and policy research to support company advocacy is commonly commissioned. It is useful for corporate affairs leadership to authorise or be a clearing house for the appointment of external consultants and be active in their appointment and supervision.

Where there is limited scale and therefore limited resources, for example in small operations or branches in small overseas economies, only 'fly-in' corporate affairs support from the corporate centre will be justified.

INTERNATIONAL CORPORATE AFFAIRS

In a disparate but highly connected world, corporate affairs has a role in ensuring consistency and cohesion in global policy and can assist in minimising surprises in the non-market environment.

Different challenges arise in various stages or forms of international activity including the consideration of market entry, relationships with joint venture partners, sourcing product, and ongoing management of corporate affairs in established businesses.

There are many relevant factors to consider when entering new markets. They include: potential impacts of global geopolitical developments; power structures in target countries; the stability of the political process; the predictability of laws affecting business; reliability of institutions like the legal system; possible corruption in business practices; and the risk of civil and social unrest. Joint ventures with local companies, sometimes mandated by host governments, assist in adapting to local mores and expectations, but companies can be damaged by any problems with their partners' behaviour, reputation and affiliations.

Traditionally, political risk assessment was undertaken by a 'grand tour' whereby executives visited countries to check conditions and 'get a feel' for the environment. This is usually accompanied by counsel from individuals with longstanding or close familiarity with a country. Firms also rely heavily on the analysis of external risk consultants, banks and insurance companies. Embassies can provide useful guidance and, in some cases, will assist companies with host governments. In reality, a mixture of all of these methods is the norm.

As corporate affairs teams are skilled in social and political environmental analysis, it is appropriate for them to be engaged early when a company is considering entry in a new market. In one example, corporate affairs was asked to undertake country screenings and advise on socio-political matters before any line manager could take an investment proposal to the board. In another example, a government relations executive was seconded from corporate affairs to a team working on an international infrastructure bid. Political risk work by corporate affairs has not been common in Australia but is increasingly becoming part of its role.

A key requirement of managing corporate affairs across business units internationally is to maintain global cohesion and reputation while being responsive to the realities of local environments. In addition to variations in local cultures that need to be understood and responded to, foreign governments and local business partners can have different values and policy priorities in such areas as the environment; diversity and gender equity; relationships in local politics; business practices; and labour issues in the supply chain. Apart from the need for consistency with corporate values, activists, with their pervasive global networks and sophisticated use of social media, are effective in holding companies to their principled claims wherever they operate. Accordingly, it is important for companies to have clear statements of purpose and standards and disciplines to ensure compliance across geographies while adapting the mandates of parent companies to local circumstances.

Increasingly, expatriate Westerners have been replaced by local corporate affairs staff who are best positioned to build local networks, work with local language media, relate to various stakeholders, understand nuances that may be missed by translators, and interpret the intricacies of local politics. They help to mitigate the cultural clashes caused by uneducated or insensitive company executives who have been 'parachuted in' from another country.

Matrix reporting is particularly challenging in many international

Community Investment – Horses for Courses

A proprietary study by the Allen Consulting Group of the community investment strategies of seven global Western companies in eight Asian countries demonstrated the need for local variations. In all cases, securing local government support and a licence to operate, while maintaining consistency with their global corporate community investment philosophy, drove their program choices. Unilever, for example, with its international programs supporting public health and development, provided floating medical clinics to service remote areas and provided capital and product micro-businesses in small villages in Bangladesh; IBM focused on school education; and Motorola on technological development in universities. Several companies partnered with government agencies in community welfare initiatives or, for example in Vietnam, communist party-sponsored charities. To build government support, one company provided a customs agency with technology to prevent the smuggling of a competitive product. In a fiercely nationalist country, an American fast-food company supported local communities while hiding its national identity behind a local partner. In a neighbouring country, where customers wanted a Western experience, it emphasised its American ownership front and centre in community investment and other programs.

company structures. A corporate affairs practitioner may have a reporting line to a country manager, one or more business units in a country, as well as to the head of global corporate affairs. This can lead to duplication of effort and the need to manage different expectations and priorities.

Approaches to achieving coordination and building a cohesive global community of practice in corporate affairs vary across companies but commonly include regular structured conference calls; annual global meetings; visits of distributed staff to head office; and secondments or working together on international projects. These meetings and secondments are also valuable in providing training and professional development.

Fly-in fly-out practitioners to manage corporate affairs can be the only option when companies have enterprises in small economies or small distributed business units where scale does not permit a local corporate affairs presence. Country managers or business operators are called upon to undertake many of the functions of corporate affairs but with little experience of dealing with government and other complex stakeholders. In this case, communications links with the international corporate affairs practice are important and some professional development is desirable.

FUNCTION MEASUREMENT

Measurement is becoming increasingly important over the years as corporate affairs departments seek to quantify what they are getting for investment in them. At the same time, boards and leadership teams want evidence of corportae affairs' contributions to meeting company goals and to justify demands on resources. Reputation measures are also increasingly embedded in executive remuneration scorecards. The value of corporate affairs is difficult to measure because its contribution is often not apparent, being intermediated through other managers, and out of the functions' control. Corporate affairs outcomes are constrained or enhanced by the behaviours of line management. Many of its activities deliver intangible outcomes, making attribution of success or failure tenuous.

In addition, investment in corporate affairs provides long-term results, timeframes beyond many other business activities. Building organisational reputation, community trust, sustainable relationships and a stakeholder-aware organisational culture is a long-term task of both tangible and intangible value. While these results can take years of sustained effort to generate, they can be lost in hours by inappropriate actions of others in the organisation.

Finally, many corporate affairs achievements are invisible to the organisation. Common examples include the mitigation of issues behind the scenes or preventing a hostile media story from appearing or reducing its negative impact. A common problem has been judging the performance of media managers by the ratio of positive to negative stories when a company is deserving bad press.

Notwithstanding difficulties, in most companies measurement is expected in every branch of management and most functions have tangible measurement tools.

The increasing focus on measurement reflects the establishment of accepted methodologies such as RepTrak for reputation measurement; the percieved value of research in effective targeting and message development (a learning from politics); and the abundance of data now available as audiences shift to digital and social media.

Apart from demonstrating that the benefits of corporate affairs outweighs its costs, particularly at budget time, measurement is also needed to assess which activities should be expanded or reduced, how activities should change to improve effectiveness, and it helps identify staff training and development needs.

Techniques common in other parts of a business have some limited value. Some corporate affairs tasks lend themselves to quantitative measures, like those based on business process engineering. Those techniques can be applied to event management or communications vehicles such as press releases or speech writing cycle times.

Most companies have established quantitative or qualitative key performance indicators (KPIs) for departments and for all levels of management from the CEO down. These are specified criteria against which performance and often individual remuneration is assessed. Qualitative KPIs can also play a role in corportae affairs management.

Benchmarking is a common tool the function uses to measure performance, processes and resource use, and to compare those factors with other companies. General management, unfamiliar with the function's shape and appropriate scale, sometimes seeks benchmaking to gain reassurance about their company's use of resources or activities compared to others. Done well, the technique helps to identify improvements and the ways they can be implemented.

However, benchmarking alone does not demonstrate the important relationship between corporate affairs performance and its value to the organisation. Only when conducted through a series of longitudinal projects can it be seen as a key element in ongoing routine performance measurement.

Intangible products of good performance, but arguably the most valuable, are costs the company avoided and opportunities for the company that are created by corporate affairs contributions. These are achieved as a result of many of the function's activities including its contribution to strategic planning. Other chapters demonstrate the non-tangible value to business success of such things as a good reputation, constructive stakeholder relations, government and regulator support, and the cooperation and support of employees. Costs saved and opportunities created by shorter project development times (stakeholder relations), access to resources (positive reputation) and regulatory wins (government relations) can significantly impact financial return.

Most measures of the function's performance will necessarily be qualitative, most commonly surveys of internal and external stakeholders. Surveys can take many forms to elicit responses from communty stakeholders, government actors and staff, as well as feedback on the contribution of corporate affairs from others in management. To ensure the frankest possible feedback, surveys of external respondents are usually best conducted by third-party providers.

Criteria for the measurement of performance should be based on a clear understanding of corporate affairs objectives and success in achieving those objectives, rather than identifying and counting activities undertaken. Accordingly, it has been useful to consider categories of measurement as inputs, outputs and outcomes. Inputs are the resources consumed in the production of outputs. They are the easiest but least valuable things to measure. Outputs are the result of inputs such as products or services. They can include the number of issues managed, speeches written or interest groups contacted.

Outcomes are the benefits produced as a result of the inputs and outputs. Outcome measurement shifts the focus from activities to results, from how a program or activity operates to the good it accomplishes. It records the extent to which a project or activity caused changes in a desired direction. They are the hardest variable to measure but the most valuable.

The distinction between inputs, outputs and outcomes can be illustrated by examining them in corporate affairs sub-functions.

In government realtions, inputs might be the number of meetings with government targets, the number and quality of submissions or issues papers prepared, or the monitoring of regulatory developments. Outputs might include contributions to analysis and policy development, decision-maker attention to submissions, and education or engagement of line management. Outcomes might be positive regulatory changes or the anticipation of emerging regulatory challenges.

For issues management, typical input measures might include developing an issues management system, documenting and distributing issues briefs, or maintaining databases. Output measures could be internal customer satisfaction, number of issues managed, and senior management buy-in to the issues process. Outcome measures might include saving compliance costs, anticipating regulatory change, or resolving an issue in a timely manner.

For employee communications, inputs could be the the number of meetings held with staff and timely management of intranet and newsletters. Outputs could be the reach of messages, engagement in internal social media, or effective management of corporate information and knowledge. Outcomes could be staff understanding of business priorities and direction – most commonly measured through annual engagement surveys and other pulse surveys – a positive perception of the company as employer of choice, or acceptance of an ambassadorial role for the company.

The definition of corporate affairs roles in job descriptions is important. A narrow focus on tasks rather than outcomes can influence the mindset of incumbents. Job descriptions can also impact job evaluation (and appropriate levels of remuneration) assesed by HR or salary consultants. It is hard to appreciate the levels of judgment and experience required of corportate affairs managers and the the complexity of the environments in which they work if job descriptions focus solely on tasks and processes, ignoring their strategic role and expected impact.

CORPORATE AFFAIRS COMPETENCIES

A variety of backgrounds can lead to careers in corporate affairs. Some executives have made successful transitions from general management and a number who have started their careers in corporate affairs have been appointed CEOs and chairs of major companies. One became Australia's 28th governor-general.

Corporate affairs employees often come from the ranks of government and politics. Most commonly, they have served as staff advisors to ministers. However, in some cases, politicians, including cabinet ministers and even a former state premier, have transitioned from politics to corporate affairs roles. One notable example is Sir Nicholas Clegg, a former UK deputy prime minister who became the head of corporate affairs for Facebook, now Meta Platforms.

A background in politics provides a deep understanding of government processes and insight into how issues arise and are addressed by the political and regulatory systems. It may also bring valuable contacts.

It is important however that those with political backgrounds do not allow ideological agendas or party politics to intrude on their corporate work. It is also important to understand the differences between the approach and instruments of political strategy and that of corporate affairs. One significant distinction is that politics in Western democracies tends to be a zero-sum game. It is driven by the negative stereotyping of opponents and their positions whereas corporate affairs is much more nuanced, often needing empathy and understanding of those with different perspectives. It is normally in the interests of companies to seek collaboration and the 'sweet spot' between corporate interests and those of the community that enable their business pursuits. Another important difference is the timeframes of politics and business. Parliamentary offices prioritise short-term gains from daily wins and upcoming elections. While market pressures do necessitate short-term business results and some issues have demanding timeframes, businesses focus more on long-term social licence and performance over an investment cycle.

Associations need the same approach as corporate affairs practitioners in this regard. One controversial industry association under pressure hired a former senior party apparatchik to help the industry out of a reputation crisis. They followed his recommendations into a political campaign using shock jocks and political-style advertising, a strategy that backfired, exacerbating their issues. A number of high-profile politicians who have become association CEOs have had to make this adjustment.

Journalism is a major source of recruits to the profession. Those in the media often have an interest and broad understanding of the social and political environment and how it is seen by diverse communities. They tend to be intellectually curious and are trained to be articulate. Writing, editing and other forms of communication are central to all corporate affairs' roles. In addition to technical skills, journalists understand how both formal messages and the informal body language of organisations are conveyed and perceived in the media and beyond.

There is regular movement between companies and industry associations, which often recruit from the same pool, including former ministers, senior bureaucrats, and journalists. Industry associations can be seen as corporate affairs departments representing their industries, requiring similar competencies.

Changes in the function have led to opportunities for employees with other backgrounds including law and psychology. The growth of sustainability issues within the function beyond the promotion of ESG issues, and the need for digital and social media skills have led to appointments of those with specialist expertise.

Roles are available for base grade entry in some companies but entrants to corporate affairs are more often recruited after a period working in government, communications agencies or not-for-profit organisations.

There are examples of successful transitions from general management and other staff functions like marketing when recruits have relevant interests and aptitudes. The most important of these is intellectual curiosity and a deep interest in politics and society. The function is relied upon to follow and interpret politics, public policy developments, public sentiment, evolving societal values, and the impact of global trends and geopolitical developments. This requires a focus on learning and an appetite for appropriating a wide variety of information sources. As discussed in Chapter 7, self-awareness and the capacity for empathetic listening to diverse opinions is essential for successful engagement with a complex range of stakeholders.

Another important aptitude is the tolerance for ambiguity and imprecision. This quality is not always prevalent in other corporate professions, where a single correct answer and scientific logic often dominate. The dynamic social systems of human society require nuance and differ from the fixed systems of the physical world. This may be why some of the most successful practitioners have a liberal arts education.

Some observers have characterised the function as 'the conscience of the organisation' but conscience cannot be delegated. It is the responsibility of all managers to act ethically and advocate ethical practice. Allocating the role of 'conscience' to corporate affairs implies a sort of separation from other members of the executive team and an assumption of special moral insight, much like manufacturers who create a head of quality role for production lines when all managers should be responsible for quality. Corporate affairs can, however, enhance ethical clarity within executive teams by highlighting community standards and expectations, as well as drawing attention to negative social impacts. Its job is much easier when the entire company is sensitive to ethical issues relevant to organisational activity.

While a deep understanding of the non-market environment is the key to success in the function, its leading practitioners must be seen internally and externally to understand and be authoritative on the basic business drivers of the company and to speak its language. This requires the function to have a working knowledge of a company's finance, technologies, competitors, market situation and key business objectives and strategies. It is important to be 'business savvy'. Business literacy is also essential for corporate affairs managers to be accepted as an integral part of leadership teams, with the licence to contest ideas with other senior managers.

The ability to provide negative feedback and fearless advice stems from being respected. However, when pointing out social or political risks, practitioners may be viewed as constraints on the plans of line managers and can potentially be perceived as negative influences within the management team. This sets up negative tension between their departments. Diplomacy and sensitivity are also required when pushing back against internal requests for support when resources are not available. Or when they compete with clearly established plan priorities.

Corporate affairs managers often have to juggle and synthesise a wide range of factors within compressed timelines in an increasingly pressured and heightened operating environment. The complexity and multifaceted nature of the function requires practitioners to manage numerous simultaneous tasks and to effectively prioritise them. Important too is self-confidence and the ability to stay calm in a storm and maintain perspective when other managers are experiencing pressure and stress.

An understanding of evolving technology is increasingly critical. This alone may accelerate the retirement of more seasoned professionals who do not fully embrace the benefits that technology can offer.

ACKNOWLEDGEMENTS

I would like to thank the senior corporate affairs practitioners who generously contributed their comments in the writing of this book: Jane Anderson, Christian Bennett, Luke Botting, Gerard Brown, David Byers, Jean Carvalho, Tim Duncan, Paul Edwards, Lauren Fragapane, John Galligan, Emily Gatt, Professor Jenn Griffin, Fruzsina Hasanyi, Rob Hadler, Troy Hey, Jason Laird, Alexis Lindsay, George Littlewood, Rob Lomdahl, Kym Lynch, Liz McNamara, Melanie McMillan, Mathew Percival, Doug Pinkham, Elle Pound, Ann Raleigh, Samantha Stevens, David Stewart and Tricia Wunch.

Executive director Wayne Burns and his staff at the Centre for Corporate Public Affairs have helped in many ways and supported this project.

I am grateful for the academics in the field who have influenced and encouraged me over my journey including Professors Ed Freeman, Charles Fombrun, Jenn Griffin, John Mahon, James Post and Pete Sandman. And to Professors Phil Harris and Craig Fleischer, editors of various publications, who encouraged me to keep thinking and writing.

Georgie Raik-Allen and Romy Moshinsky from Real Publishing provided their invaluable editorial expertise to ensure the clarity of the text. Thanks also to designer Marianna Berek-Lewis for her important contribution to the book's presentation.

Finally, thank you to my partner Christine Hubay for tolerating my distraction on this project.

INDEX